I0876694

## Praise for *What a House Can Hold*

"Laura Childs Gill writes with such a command of her narrative weave, that we are hooked by the story itself—the quest for a home place and the fearless exploration of loves lost and found—and at the same time amazed by the artistic joinery we see happening at every turn. To her title *What a House Can Hold*—my response is 'much more than I would have thought.'"
—Sven Birkerts, author of *The Miro Worm and the Mysteries of Writing*

"*What a House Can Hold* is not so much a book as a door opening upon a quickening, vivid heart. It is tender, complex and erudite; a feast of symbols and a dispatch on the nexus of love and writing. I did not want it to end."
—Sue Rainsford, author of *Follow Me to Ground*

"Lyrical and deeply hopeful, *What a House Can Hold* is a story for anyone who has wondered whether home is less a destination than a way of holding oneself. It asks what we carry, what we remember, and what remains after loss rearranges the rooms of a life. It is a book about memory held with care, the lives we inherit and the loves that echo through them. Blending interior reflection with history, art, food, and travel, this tender work never closes itself off. Even in its most personal moments, it leaves the door open for the reader to enter, recognize themselves, and stay awhile."
—Shauna Barbosa, author of *Cape Verdean Blues*

"Sharply honest and artfully structured, *What a House Can Hold* considers not only the aftereffects of endings and beginnings, but the indelible impact of moments lived between. In these clear-eyed and compelling essays, a marriage dissolves, much-loved cities are parted

with, familiar versions of self are tested. 'No one means to lose anything,' observes Gill, who invites us to ask what we're allowed to want when it comes to connection and fulfillment. A terrific rendering of separation and self-renewal, *What a House Can Hold* is a radiant debut that marks Gill as a writer of patient observation and marked intelligence."
—Shara Lessley, author of *The Explosive Expert's Wife*

"Bold, rigorous, and beautifully constructed, *What a House Can Hold* is a remarkable collection. Laura Childs Gill writes about the mysteries of longing, loss, and connection in ways that left me spellbound. I loved this book."
—Chelsea Hodson, author of *Tonight I'm Someone Else*

# What a House Can Hold

Laura Childs Gill

Autofocus Books
Easton, Pennsylvania

Published by Autofocus Books
autofocusbooks.com

Essays/Literature
ISBN: 978-1-957392-51-6
Library of Congress Control: 2026938960

Cover design by Amy Wheaton

For B.

# Contents

# What a House Can Hold

## Beginnings: A Series of Attempts

This is a love story that begins with a single question:

"Do you want to have a beer tonight?"

***

This is a love story from a person who always hated when other people fell in love.

The first was my older sister. In middle school, she had a crush on a boy with big blue eyes and moppy, blonde-ish hair. I hated everything about him. I also thought he was cute. When he was around, she became strange. She tried to be with him alone. She tried to make him laugh. She did not want me anywhere close. One night, when he was over, I wrote him a letter. I told him that he should get away. He should stop kissing my sister. She was mine.

***

This isn't just a love story from a person who always hated when people fell in love but a person who had strong opinions about what love should look like.

My cousin and I dated step-brothers in seventh grade, and I remember that she kissed hers with a passion that sometimes made me feel confused. When me and mine kissed, we were calmer. Perhaps it could not even be called "kissing." Our mouths held back from hunger. We liked to hold hands most of all, and this, I thought, made our love stronger. All the touching was a performance, I decided; the groping around for one another's bodies indicated a love that would never last.

How did I learn to be afraid of what the body desired? Or was it that my body did not have desire?

***

"Do you want to have a beer tonight?"

"Yes."

***

Nothing I own is in D.C. anymore.

It's hard to begin with an inaccurate statement.

***

There are items I own in D.C.

After a recent trip there, I left two pairs of earrings and a water bottle, and I have a feeling some other items remain: books perhaps, socks maybe, and potentially kitchenware. Some of those items were ours, not mine, and I am not sure if that counts.

There is definitely a tote bag with a photo album inside, which my ex-husband, M., tried to give me on another trip to D.C. The album was supposedly the last remnant from the house we owned together. He rightfully assumed I'd be at a friend's party that weekend, so he brought the item there. But I'd left an hour earlier to meet a friend for a panicked beer. It wasn't him I was panicked about seeing, it was all the friends and former acquaintances I'd already seen: they'd multiplied by at least one offspring, if not two, in the years since I'd left.

When I was not there, he gave the bag to a friend, who tried to give it to me the next day. I said I couldn't take it with me on the plane, so I left the bag with a different friend who doesn't give anything away; her house is filled with old posters, picture collages, new jeans she'll never wear, and enough art supplies to fill a Michaels.

***

When I first moved to Miami, M. sent me a box of items from the house to get me started in my new life: a wool blanket, three bowls, a frying pan, framed photographs, and a plastic cutting board. The objects were seemingly thrown together in a rush, but there was also a conscientiousness about the choices—most of the items were mine before our relationship or purchases my friends and family had made for our wedding.

I was both moved and slightly hurt as I opened the box. As I went through, I noticed the items were not just ones my friends had gifted but also some of our cheapest items, both in cost and sentimentality. But there was also a real kindness to his sending it; I didn't ask for anything, hadn't asked for anything, and I left in such a terrible, slow, disoriented rush (how can you rush slowly? I'll teach you) that he could have simply thrown me, and everything I owned, away.

***

They say mice chew off their legs to save their bodies. I've never seen it, but apparently it's true: they gnaw at their thin bones in an effort to stay alive.

The summer I was not-yet-separated-but-in-retrospect-separating from M., I sometimes lived in the barn behind my mother's house and contended with mice. The debate was always the same: was I happier to let them live, contorting my face as I reached to clear their droppings out of corners each morning, or was I happier killing them and dealing with a dead mouse on a trap? I'd never seen just legs. All I'd ever encountered were the bodies: small and smashed.

"It's horrible!" my dad would yell when I told him. "Get the poison!"

My mother did not approve. "It doesn't just kill the mouse but the owl who eats it," she said. I imagined a sea of dead owls all over the meadow, and I couldn't bring myself to do it.

Instead, I lived in an in-between state—some nights, I let the mice run free; other nights, I used the traps. Often, I didn't sleep in the barn but instead walked to my mother's house where there were still mice, but only one at a time, and they were my mother's to contend with. Those days, I would use the barn as a place to write and pretend: *if I couldn't see them dead or alive, they did not exist.*

***

My grandfather on my father's side began his most famous book, *Here at The New Yorker,* with: "Happy writers have histories shorter even than happy families." He also loved the first line of the New Testament: "In the beginning was the word."

My father began his most famous book, *How Starbucks Saved My Life,* with: "This is the true, surprising story of an old white man who was kicked out of the top of the American Establishment. . . and came to learn what is important in life."

Mine might begin:

Writers shorten histories.

***

Writers only know how to begin.

***

I could start with my name. It's a prompt I give to my students: *what's in a name?* They often tell me they don't know; they often say they were named after someone they never met. One student of mine was named Brooklyn, and when I asked if there was some connection to the place, she said no. When I pushed further—

*did your parents meet in Brooklyn? are they from Brooklyn?*—she rolled her eyes: "It has nothing to do with Brooklyn. They just liked the name."

My mother also says she "just liked the name" Laura. One of her best friends, my godmother, was named Laura, and she asked her if she liked her name, and she said yes, and so there it was, there it is: Laura. She named my sister and brother after family members. My sister shares a name with our aunt and both grandmothers. My brother shares his with an uncle, my father, and our great-great-grandfather, who was kind of a big deal.

***

Is that the beginning?

Does it start with my great, great grandfather (how many greats can you go on for? How many can you add, to truly get to the beginning?), who helped found General Electric? It is a detail I am not as interested in as what he said about electricity—or, to be more accurate, what he said Edison said about electricity: "There are only two things in the world and electricity is the other one. One is matter. The other is this unknown something which makes matter move."

If I'm honest, I sometimes even forget exactly how I am related to him. I forget where he lived (Lynn, Massachusetts) and how he started his career (shoes). And yet, nothing happens without him, not really, not actually, because in graduate school my professor told us that every story is about money and so perhaps the money, and where it comes from, is the start of the story. But I repeatedly have to look the details up because I can't remember how he helped found General Electric and what role he played. Sometimes, I can't even always remember his full name. I just googled it to check: Charles Albert Coffin.

There is no privilege like the privilege of forgetting.

***

Donald Hall destroyed my marriage.

***

Donald Hall wrote an essay that destroyed my marriage.

***

Donald Hall wrote many essays about marriage, and he had two marriages, which he accompanied with three beards, but the essay that I could not shake was his essay about the "third thing" in marriage. He wrote that every marriage needs one: a time when the couple comes together in "double attention." He said the "third thing" can be "John Keats, or the Boston Symphony Orchestra, or Dutch interiors, or Monopoly," but by the time I read the essay, I could only see the "third thing" as what was missing between M. and me; our third thing was a lack of a third thing, even though I can now see that for years we'd had many third things—friends, food, travel, a home. Donald Hall did write that sometimes "you lose a third thing," but he did not say that sometimes one person finds another person in graduate school with whom they discover a third thing that overwhelms and transforms them, so much so that they can no longer see anything except that which is connected to the new person, the new version of them, the new third thing.

***

"Do you want to have—"

***

This is the actual beginning of an essay I published, which I thought was the start of this book:

*People go to Emily Dickinson's house for all kinds of reasons, most of which include a desire to see the room where she famously wrote poems one might want to write someday.*

But I didn't know then that this was not the start of the story. The book was about traveling around to authors' houses, looking for answers. I had deluded myself into thinking that I wasn't a person ruining my marriage; instead, I was a writer, someone who went on trips and wrote about them for the public eye. I did not say: I have fallen in love with someone. I did not say: *This love has jostled my entire system; I no longer know what direction I am headed.* I said: I went to Emily Dickinson's house and thought it was strange—now, I will go to many other author's houses and write about how strange they are because authors and their homes and our attachments to them might just give me the solution to the problem I am having with wanting to be an author and struggling to be at home.

***

I've been told at various points in my life I have nothing to be sad about. I think these people are sometimes right. I have also been told I could simply think differently, and then I would not be sad. I think those people are sometimes right, too.

Before I could google "how to be less sad," I sought guidance from teachers, family, and friends, and I was always hoping for a religion, book, or guru to sweep me away. My middle school days in a choir had set me up to feel transcendence in sacred music, and my high school friends had set me up to listen to the music of The Roots and Toots and the Maytals and read the books of Thích Nhất Hạnh and Don Miguel Ruiz. There was also a book my sister and I read and loved and felt was sacred: *Gift from the Sea* by Anne Morrow Lindbergh. In it, she writes about how every shell she encounters on the beach holds a metaphor for how one should live one's life. It was a book I loved and then later quickly dismissed as cheesy. I now go back to read the introduction and see neither of those; I see a woman on the brink.

***

I owned the house in D.C. with M. until recently. I hadn't lived there in years and hadn't paid the mortgage, but it was still, in a way, mine.

On my last trip to the house, I was there to try to remove everything I owned. M. had put the items all together in the basement, and I had invited some friends to help. One friend came and simply talked to me while I did the work of picking through and organizing what was there. This friend who came to talk to me had just had her first experience with feelings outside of her marriage. They were big feelings, and they were feelings that never got named, and they were feelings she ultimately decided to move on from for the sake of her marriage. I could tell she was still holding on—a part of her was sad to let go—and as I heard her discuss her decision, I could not disconnect from my own. I knew the push and the pull, and I knew that whatever decision she made, all the pieces and shards would stay inside her, and she would have to say goodbye to each one.

She talked as I went through bags M. had thrown together. There were jackets and bras and what now can only be called souvenirs from our wedding: cards, paper flowers, saved invitations, programs, and photographs. Those were placed with other memorabilia from our life together—a blown-up photograph from a 30th birthday party and posters from another party M. organized for me on Rehoboth Beach. He'd also brought down all of my books from the two bookshelves he'd made for me. One of brick and wood with live edges, the other a floating shelf he built as I began pulling away.

On our wedding day, we'd had people write notes of advice. The friend who came over to talk to me had written her advice with her husband. They said to keep the marriage at the center, to treat the marriage like its own person. There were the two of us, yes, but there was also now a marriage, and it needed just as much care and attention as anyone.

I always appreciated that advice. The message resonated for me because I believed that M. and I were good at just that: keeping our togetherness central. Our strength was what we built alongside one another, beyond ourselves. Our relationship was sturdy because it held the both of us, and the both of us were different. I'd go on to read articles and books that would reiterate this message about relationships. Their claims were: you are not to find a soulmate but to instead find the person with whom your soul can be free. I was reassured. I had done that; I had achieved. I had finally figured out how to be.

***

One of the jokes circling around the graduate program was that it would destroy your life. *Ha. Ha.* What confused me about the joke was that, presumably, those who had chosen a low-residency program did so for the same reasons as me: to stay in their life. But the joke was ever present, or, perhaps, it was the lore created by those who wanted to believe it was a true, almost desired effect of the program: in some dramatic way, your life would change. Either you would realize your job was a sham or your marriage was unsatisfactory or the city you were living in was stifling *all that creativity,* and it would spit you out in new parts.

My assumption was that the change would happen fast. If you were a person who needed a change, the residency factory would see it right away; they'd take you, introduce you to some writer, some faculty member, some student in your cohort, and boom:

there'd go your life. I did not imagine you could make jokes about the phenomenon for a year and a half—that you could ask, "Do you want to have a beer tonight?" without any care for your life to change—all to be spit out years later in an apartment near the beach. Transformations were not meant to be slow and tottering. They were meant to be sudden, like Gregor's. One morning you go to sleep a cog in the wheel and the next day, you wake up a bug.

***

When I officially separated from M., I moved to an apartment next to the ocean. My mother was baffled. "You've never been an ocean person," she said. She was right. I wasn't an ocean person, and I wasn't a beach person either. And yet, I moved blocks away from the sea to settle at the moment I felt most unsettled.

A friend who'd separated from her fiancé came to visit soon after. She said she was going to do a water ritual. She would take everything she was carrying with her into the sea and leave it there for the water to devour.

***

In high school, a biology teacher taught us about the chemistry of water. She said there was a scientific reason why it felt so good to shower. When she explained the chemistry to us, she rubbed her hands all over her arms and legs as she expressed its power: "Isn't it delicious?"

Most of us hadn't yet accessed our own pleasure, let alone considered hers. We giggled as she touched her body. We squirmed. We distanced ourselves from her rapture.

***

My family likes to describe a simple break in my personality. Growing up, I was a happy child, perhaps even sometimes deemed "the happiest." I was the baby who giggled, napped, ate, entertained, and easily went with anyone, anywhere. I was drawn particularly to men, and, within that category, men with beards. This is what I am told. I was a happy baby, even a happy child, until we moved to Norfolk, Connecticut.

What was there to be unhappy about?

I grew up in L.A. with an older sister I worshiped and a younger brother I loved. Some days, when I woke up in the mornings, my father would make us breakfast: Honey Nut Cheerios with extra honey drizzled on top. Every afternoon after school, I came home and had the same snack: a bagel with a piece of American cheese toasted to perfection. The first plant I learned to name was the Honeysuckle, and I learned to name it because I loved to stick my nose right into it. I knew we were near home when we got off the exit and passed the lady selling flowers from a bucket. Or was it fruit? Fresh pomegranates grew from trees in our yard, and I loved opening the skin to see the hundreds of gathered seeds.

***

This is a love story that doesn't have a clear beginning. Or if it does, it is the kind that stays hovering long before it knows when to land.

***

B. and I didn't talk much during the first few days of graduate school. I knew him as the person who was standing in the back during orientation. He was funny, and he was honest. He said he didn't really have a clue what he was doing there because he was a visual artist and already had a masters in that. The room laughed. I think that is what he said, but I don't exactly remember. After that, I didn't see him for days.

What I said that morning I remember even less, but I do remember that the program director prodded me into mentioning my grandfather. "Oh, and my grandfather was Brendan Gill," I said, "he wrote for *The New Yorker*." Once I said it, there were some nods of recognition, even one extremely enthusiastic, "Wait, really?" but mostly, no one responded at all. I was embarrassed. Not just because his name was no longer recognizable to many but because even if it had been, I wouldn't have known what to say. I wanted to align myself with him, but in my life to date, I hadn't. I was an English teacher living in Washington, D.C. I had never read many, if any, of his books. *The New Yorker* often sat unread on my bedside table.

***

The first piece I wrote for my very first graduate school workshop was a short, five-page series of vignettes about breaks and fissures: real, metaphorical, and imagined. The piece stood out not for its excellence but because it was so short, so unfinished, and so much "not an essay." I had taken the program's directive literally—*bring in something that needs work, bring something in that is unfinished*—but most people had brought in either the essay they submitted in their applications or chapters of a book they were about to publish.

Everyone was kind about my scraps. They suggested I read Eula Biss and Mary Ruefle and Anne Carson and Georges Perec and John D'Agata and Maggie Nelson. Before workshop, one person reached out to me to tell me she enjoyed the piece; when I looked her up, I discovered she had published a chapbook, did performance art, and was one step away from most of the authors whose names had been suggested to me. Her attention made me feel good, if somewhat embarrassed. I was behind in every way, and I had no idea.

The vignettes would move into essays, but the feedback would often remain the same. *We need to see the narrator here; we need to understand the context to better connect with what she is going through.*

***

"Do you want to have a beer tonight?"

"Yes."

If I knew what the narrator was going through, I would not be writing to you.

***

When I met M., he was sitting on an office chair with his legs crossed. "Hello!" he said, lifting his face from the computer. He was the only one in the office who introduced himself to me. We were in the early days of the Obama campaign and every person believed in work, or believed that if they always looked like they were working, then they were doing the work. M. was relaxed. Calm. Kind. He invited me out for coffee, introduced me to his friends, and even brought me into the staff section for Obama's speech in Philadelphia, where the crowd roared and my body was covered in chills. He took off his Obama sticker and placed it below my left shoulder.

The same evening, he came to my house for a party, and he stuck by my side. I was slightly annoyed. I was not yet interested in him because I was a person who believed that love looked a particular way, and our connection was not what I imagined love to be. I had never been close to someone like him—a computer whiz turned Obama organizer turned Obama-organizing-computer-whiz who owned a cat in college, loved board games, and did not care what people thought about him. My attractions had often been to people who were performers: those who could make an entire dinner table laugh. M. was not that person; he was completely comfortable with who he was. I was disarmed.

He brought a few others from the campaign to the party, but once they left, he followed me around. The theme of the party was "flowers." We told people to dress up in their best florals and raised a small sum of money for a community garden. Most people wore outfits with flowers on them, but I had only invited the people from the campaign the day before, so they did not have enough time to pull their outfits together. M. had figured it out anyway. He wore his red USC t-shirt with a flowered logo.

The apartment was packed with people dancing in the basement and trying to have conversations in the kitchen. I'd just been dumped by a person I thought would never dump me because he had pursued me so aggressively. He was about to arrive. I was also being touched more than I wanted to be touched by an old friend from college, who, regardless of the amount of alcohol consumed, always talked as if she was drunk, her lips never quite opening over the words.

A week before, I had told her I was interested in potentially dating women. I did not want to date her, but she took it as an invitation. Throughout the evening, her hands glided across my back any time I sat near her, and she looked at me with glazed eyes and a strange smile. I wanted to leave, but I didn't know how to go: what was the code for rejecting a woman? What was the code for rejecting a man?

My ex came to the party and then left to go to our friend's house next door. I followed him. I wanted him to tell me again why it was that he dumped me, even though I knew. He had been one of the only people I'd been in a relationship with who actually had a clear reason, and it was a reason that made sense because I knew it was true. Our sexual relationship was "weird," he said. And it was. Despite being somewhat of an Adonis, I had never been very attracted to him. We rarely had sex. Instead, we talked all day over email and on the phone, and when I went over to his house, he cooked delicious, elaborate meals, after which we'd watch *It's Always Sunny in Philadelphia* and sometimes, but not often, have sex. In the mornings, he would wake up two hours before work to exercise; he had a six pack he could not lose.

M. stayed at the apartment while I went to try to win my weird-sex-ex back. He stayed there, waiting for me, and when I returned and told him I had just gone to see said ex, he did not blink an eye. He stayed over. He slept in my bed. We did not touch.

When we woke up the next morning, I was surprised he was still there, and I was surprised I was telling him not only how silly I was to try to get my ex back, but also how I wanted to go to lesbian bars that night. He did not react. He said he would see me at the office.

***

My first ever photograph on my first ever camera was a stop sign. The sign was halfway into the ground, and it was covered in vine. When I printed my photographs, I put the photograph at the front of the album, which was mostly full of pictures of friends and family save for the covered stop sign.

In high school, I was scolded for one of my albums full of people. The album had photographs of friends smiling around a bottle of vodka, me at a bar in the Bahamas with a cigarette, more friends red-faced and red-eyed and cigarette-holding: high, drunk, elated, and on the prowl, or somewhere in between. My dorm parents found the album, sent it to my house, and included a long letter. They told me their daughter had seen it and lost her respect for me; they warned me of lung cancer and an early death.

Before I left for Spain between freshman and sophomore year of college, I gifted my friends a photocopied image of myself alongside a letter. The image was the one the college had taken for my ID during the first week. In it, I looked like I had been sent to prison. I was mid-tears. By the end of the year, I'd made friends. I wrote to them alongside photocopies of my grumpy face; I thanked them for helping to right the frown—I wrote to them that their friendship had made all the difference.

When I left, I went to Spain for half the year. A friend gave me a hat his mother had sewn for him. He asked me not to lose it. I spent the fall taking photographs of the hat around Granada; on a car in front of a graffitied wall, on a fence, on a park bench. I was back to being lonely and sad, and the hat was my new way of highlighting that sadness. By the time I came home and packed my bag to return, the hat was gone.

During the years I was falling in love with B., I was drawn both to what was abandoned and what was becoming. A jacket on a bench, a Miller High Life in a pile of leaves, shoes on the beach, flowers taking over fences, grass growing through cracks in the sidewalk, vines covering telephone wires. In moments, I thought I was using photographs to disassociate from my own experience; only now am I able to see the ways in which they depicted it. In *On Photography*, Susan Sontag writes about the camera as a violent object: pointed towards you, always at the ready, taking in what you do and do not want to see again.

***

You take photographs of something you know you are going to lose.

***

You take photographs of what you want to remember.

***

I turned my body towards B., and then he asked: "Can I put my arm around your shoulders?" When he rubbed his thumb on my arm, I told him, "No, not that." *It was too much,* I said to him. *The pleasure is too much,* I said to myself.

A week later, the emails started. One a day. Two a day. Four a day. Sometimes, ten. Emails then GChat then an attempt at

Snapchat and Duo and often FaceTime; then layovers; then made up trips; then more emails and more WhatsApp messages and more video calls and more and more and more—sometimes in the middle of the night, frequently in the morning, and most often in the afternoons, in the space between work and home, where our relationship lived: our voices in one another's cars talking about someday—matching tattoos and artist talks and collaborations and trips, and our before days: first kisses, first loves, our favorite sweatshirts, grandparents, small towns, discovering writing, deciding to take ourselves seriously, deciding we didn't know who we were when we thought we knew who we might be.

***

The truth is that my dad knew before I did. The summer after I fell in love with B., quit my job, and decided to travel here, there, and everywhere as a way to move through and avoid the pain of what I was experiencing, I told my father I was going to Maine to see a friend. I told him that these were the types of trips I wanted to take because they were the kinds of trips I was not able to take while I was teaching. I was excited, I said, to be out in the wilderness.

*You are going alone?* he wondered. I still lived with M., still shared a home with M., still was married to M. Throughout our entire relationship, I rarely traveled without him. I'd developed a fear of driving because he always drove. I had not told my father about my fear of driving or about B., but he seemed to understand something was amiss.

He asked: *Was M. coming?* No, I said, I was going on my own, and I was excited! I'd get to adventure out into the woods to see my friend and her husband in a place where no one could find me! I wouldn't have electricity or the internet. It would be great to have the quiet, and the peace. He told me I must be going insane.

I sort of was.

***

When my father told us about his years-long affair, we had a family meeting in the dining room. It lasted less than thirty minutes. My father told us what had happened, and then asked for questions, of which there were very few. Before the family meeting, I'd guessed that he was going to tell us he had terminal cancer, so when he told us about the affair, there was a sense of relief, which I now see was shock, too, and a slight degree of horror.

I made myself toast that morning. I can't remember if anyone else had food. As the discussion continued, I could not eat. I felt nauseous. I told my sister. "It's because you didn't toast the bread enough," she said.

As my father spoke, words appeared in my head. They said, "Yes, of course this happened." They said, "I forgive you." The toast hardened in front of me. At the end of the conversation, my mother said, "It's time to pack up for the beach."

I went upstairs, and I sat in the bathroom. I can't remember if I cried or did not cry. I do know I got myself ready to go to the lake. I do know that I did go to the lake, where we were not allowed to tell anyone what happened. I do know that as I write this now, I am surprised at just how much I do not remember, at how much I want to deny.

There was a sense of finality after the family meeting. An affair had happened. He had a son with the woman with whom he'd had an affair with (did I leave that out on the first pass?). The person he'd had an affair with was angry at him; she was harassing the family, calling aunts, my mother, and anyone who would listen. My mother had known for over a year. It was being addressed, and it would be resolved, and they would work through it together. They'd go to movies, to therapy, to dinner, to the theater. We'd go to the lake.

A year later, my father got a job at Starbucks and an apartment in Bronxville, and he never really lived at home again.

***

"This is the true, surprising story of an old white man who was kicked out of the top of the American Establishment, by chance met a young African-American woman from a completely different background, and came to learn what is important in life."

*This is the true, unsurprising story of a man who had an affair and could not bear to return to his life.*

And this?

***

I knew I was fucked when the first text from B. came through. It wasn't the first text from him ever. It was the first text from him that someone else could see. I was driving a friend from the train in New York to Connecticut. My phone was plugged into my car. The text came in across the screen, and I blushed. I think I even said, "Oh, that's a friend from grad school," to which the friend in the car said nothing, because he hadn't noticed the text to begin with.

When the message came through, I was still trying to hold onto the delusion that I had, in fact, left B. in graduate school as a friend. A collaborator. A person I would maybe send a draft of something new. But the feelings? The feelings we were going to ignore. They were too much, had been too much, and anyway, we were in the clear. We had not crossed any physical boundary—had not kissed, had barely even hugged save for a few times, and even in those times, had moved quickly through the hug (did we?), knowing if it went on any further, our bodies moving any closer, we would be screwed (we were already). We were both aware (or wanted to believe?) that even though the feelings were intense, they were likely fleeting, too. These things we'd discussed, and we decided that the more time we spent back in our lives in our already-partnered life, the more it would dissipate, the more the longings would go away.

And yet: when the text came through, my entire body buzzed. I was sure my friend had seen it: how could he not? Despite trying to split brain from body, thought from feeling, and narrative from truth, I was failing at every turn.

***

A day after the text, I panicked in the water. I was at the lake with friends—people who had, just two years earlier, come up to Norfolk for mine and M.'s wedding and at the end of the evening, swam drunk in the lake after rounds of singing and cheering: soaking wet, and in some cases, without clothes. It was the same lake we'd gone to the day my father told us about his affair. The same lake where M. had proposed. The same lake where M. had decided to fix my grandmother's sailboat years earlier, thereby solidifying himself as a member of the family, thereby becoming not just related through me but by something closer, something like blood: "He reminds me of Pop," my aunt said, "the way he is fixated on figuring out how to keep the boat afloat." It was the same lake where my grandmother would skinny dip every morning, and later in life, be wheeled in on her wheelchair, floating off and into the water seemingly without a trace of effort.

My friends were out in the middle. They'd created a flotilla of sorts with a pedalo, a canoe, tubes, and kayaks. I decided to swim towards them.

It had been just a week since I'd left B. in Vermont, and just a day after the text came through. The distance had done nothing but amplify the experience of having been close to something I had never known existed, had never known I'd never had. When I swam towards my friends, my arms grew heavy. I tried to kick my legs, and they were stuck. My heart was racing. I tried to move forward. The water was thick. By the time I made it to my friends, I could barely breathe. "Do you want to grab on?" they asked. I did.

When I recounted the story to my aunt a few days later, saying how strange it was that I felt like I could drown, she said, "but you know you can always just float, right?"

I didn't. Or I did, but my body could not because it was embodying something I had yet to discover about its new relationship to water, about its new relationship to itself. Its chemistry had been shifted for a man who was not my husband. B. was a writer, artist, friend, and then?

***

I sometimes think the beginning was this:

Our entire graduate class was together in the basement of our dorm for a makeshift party no one wanted to organize. One person walked miles through the snow to buy a bottle of Manischewitz; one person had a bottle of whiskey; I had a few beers in the fridge; B. had more, and there it was—a class party. We had people in our class in their seventies and their twenties, people who loved drinking, people who never drank and people who were disturbed by *all the drinking*: weren't we supposed to write? One woman brought Cheez Balls to the party and during every residency after, did the same, eating them and shaming herself in the same breadth: "I never do this! I can't believe I am doing this!"

The night in the basement became loud and raucous quickly; the friends I'd made were interested in keeping to themselves—they wanted to observe the scene. A part of me did too, but a part of me wanted to be near B., who was not driving the conversation nor really participating in it but close enough to it to engage with it. He was smiling often, sometimes responding to questions, often lobbing in a joke or a comment only a few people caught or understood. He was drinking a special beer, one I recognized because M. liked that beer, too. It had a thin can with a particular logo, and I knew it was delicious. I noted it, and asked him if I could have one. He said yes.

The next night, I asked: "Do you want to have a beer tonight?"

***

I saw *Fatal Attraction* when I was too young to see *Fatal Attraction*. What I learned was that affairs were bad, but women were worse.

***

If you told me this was a love story where once two people find one another, they aren't able to be together, I would tell you that this was a tragedy. But it is not a tragedy. If I told you this was a love story where two people find one another but many obstacles jump in their way, keeping them from one another for years, you might think it is a comedy. But it is not a comedy.

If it was a comedy or a tragedy, I'd know where to begin.

***

I was told affairs were not genetic when I wrote about the idea and put it in an essay I sent to a poet. I wondered if falling in love outside of a marriage was somehow imprinted in my cells. Perhaps there was some genealogical connection between my father, my grandfather, and likely many other men and women in my family and me? The poet read the essay and said no. Affairs were as common as shingles, scoliosis, hemorrhoids, broken bones, and hangnails, all of which I'd had and all of which I'd, to very varying degrees, taken little solace in knowing just how common they were. Perhaps the gene is not one that leads to affairs, I now think, but is instead a gene about how we address ruptures, which is to say: avoid them.

When we lived in L.A., my father caught his finger in the

zipper of his suitcase and ignored the pain that followed. When he came back from a business trip, it was red and purple. My mother said it was infected, and I remember being scared at the word, thinking perhaps he'd be in serious trouble. Each night, after he came back from work, my mother would make him a soaking bowl of warm water and hydrogen peroxide. He would sit at the dining room table in his suit and place his finger inside. I remember my mother saying that if he'd only addressed the injury when it happened, it would not have gotten so bad.

***

I've taught the Gárcia Márquez story, "A Very Old Man With Enormous Wings" for years, andI never remember that the very old man is discovered not at the edge of the sea but instead in a couple's courtyard. Only towards the end of the story does the sea call to him, and he starts to grow feathers on his wings. As he changes, Gárcia Márquez writes, "He must have known the reason for those changes, for he was quite careful that no one should notice them."

***

I should have known the beginning of the ending was this:

While living in D.C. with M., I kept the *New Yorker* review of *Blue Valentine* tucked in a notebook. I used it to teach movie reviews to my high school students, but I think I was also trying to teach them something else. In it, Anthony Lane writes, "Who, on the verge of growing up, would wish to learn that the first heady bloom of rapture is doomed to rot and fall?" I let the students read it and consider that question. I made them read that the film's story "is overwhelming proof that hurt is the bedfellow of love," and that "for anybody who already knows that...the film may be very hard to take."

I told them this was a good review of a great movie.

***

They said the truth would set you free.

In the beginning, this felt like a possibility.

***

"Do you want to have a beer tonight?"

"Yes."

A few minutes later, we met in the kitchen in the basement of the dormitory. I was nervous. I grabbed a Sierra Nevada and placed it on the table. We sat across from one another. Another classmate of ours came by, and he wanted to join us. We both said yes, but I remember feeling frustrated. My body tensed. I did not want this other person there. When he eventually left, I was relieved.

A year later, B. would be in D.C. for one of his gallery shows, and I would invite him to have a beer with me. I would also invite M. because it was before: before the wrist, before the blanket, before I knew anything had begun. B. and I arrived at the bar first. We sat at a table outside, our bodies practically on the sidewalk. M. arrived a few minutes later. He rode his bike right up next to us. He said hello with a big smile. Then, the feeling came again; the same one I'd had in the basement kitchen when our friend walked into the room—the one where my whole body became sturdy, heavy, and detached.

Later that night, when M. and I got home slightly buzzed and full of giggles, I suggested we go to the gallery the next day to see B.'s show. I can't remember his reaction, but we did not make a plan to see it. Perhaps a part of me knew that it would have revealed too much to be too enthusiastic about it, even though, at that time, I had no idea there was anything to reveal; perhaps another part of me, perhaps more pulsing and present, knew that I wanted to see B.'s art alone.

If the beginning is a process of chipping—the body hewing pieces of itself, and saving parts for a person it doesn't yet know—then perhaps this is the beginning. If one piece can fall away, then another can come later, and another and another, until the whole body is a set of small pieces, ready and waiting, for something to be built anew.

# House Rules

People go to Emily Dickinson's house for all kinds of reasons, most of which include a desire to see the room where she famously spent most of her time writing poems. Other people go because they are tourists, driving around Massachusetts, looking for a place to spend the afternoon. Others might happen upon it, not expecting much and quite possibly forgetting who Emily Dickinson was, save for the few facts from high school. They decide to walk in, take a tour, and leave with a Dickinson magnet.

When I went, I was going to see B.

A visit to Emily Dickinson's house is not romantic, relaxing, or private, but that's how we liked our encounters to be; neither of us was interested in the illicit components of our affair, and even the word "affair" felt disconnected from what was happening. We had been close friends and still were. And yet: we were married to other people when we met at the Dickinson house. And we were married to other people as we spent every day emailing one another. And we were married to other people when we kissed the first time, standing in a parking lot in the woods. And so, we were continuing an affair when we pulled open the screen door and entered Emily Dickinson's house together.

Immediately upon entering, a woman asked us just what exactly we were doing there. We thought it was obvious, we wanted a tour, but quickly it became clear that we'd done something wrong: did she know? Her questions kept coming. How much time did we have? Were we planning on the twelve o'clock tour? She continued to talk. She didn't know if there would be enough time to get us through the line for the tour going out that hour. Our laissez-faire attitude didn't seem to help the matter; instead, it seemed to make her upset. She looked at us. She looked at the line. And she said that she just...wasn't...sure.

We signed up for the later tour and used the hour to walk to Dickinson's grave. The weather started to shift. It was a warm, humid day, with bits of sun and dark clouds. The graveyard was across from a small shut-down strip mall, and it wasn't well-kept; the grass was overgrown, and the headstones were covered in mold.

We couldn't find it at first, and when it started to rain, we walked towards a huge tree and stood under it. Then, B. spotted the site with the fence wrapped around it. As we got closer, it seemed impossible that we could have missed her grave, which was covered in items: a lemon, pieces of paper, pens and pencils, hair elastics, and flowers. I placed the pencil I'd brought next to the others and took as many photographs as I could of the rain-soaked items. In my favorite photo, the lemon is glistening above the grave. What you can't see are the bugs grabbing my ankles. B.'s hand on my back. The sun piercing through the clouds.

The rain stuck to our clothes which stuck to our skin, and it started to become warm. We left the graveyard and made our way back when we saw a huge vulture, perched on the roof of a house. I swore it was fake, but as we got closer, we saw its head move. I nearly shuddered. It wasn't simply the largess of the bird but its contrast with the house. It might have made sense to see such a bird on an abandoned castle or a cathedral, but on a one-story white house with yellow trim, it seemed out of place. It was a stranger. It was incoherent. It was not home.

***

Later that night, B. would look up what vultures symbolize: rebirth, new beginnings, and resourcefulness. The vulture has an uncanny ability to locate death and feed itself. It asks you to rid yourself of what's not giving you life, to eat what is eating away at you.

***

We made our way back to Emily Dickinson's house where we met Steve, our serious and sentimental tour guide. His mouth quivered with every sentence, and he spoke of Dickinson as a long-lost friend rather than a famous poet he'd never met. We learned quickly from Steve what we were not allowed to do. If the Emily Dickinson house is full of anything, it is full of information about what you cannot do. You cannot take photographs inside; you cannot touch any furniture; you cannot wander on your own; when you enter the library, you can hold what might have been her pressed flowers, but you cannot really see the flowers because they are pressed between what feel like menus in your hands and so their fragility is lost—their beauty is encased in a way you cannot access; you cannot go into her room, the famous room where she was said to stay for days, writing letters and poetry—you cannot walk on its floorboards; you cannot get close enough to her dress to make out the threads holding it together, and you cannot see a single speck of dust or a handprint. You cannot.

***

People learn about Dickinson's poetry, and then they learn about what Dickinson did not do: socialize often, have children, or get married. The lore that surrounds Dickinson mostly encompasses her increased anxiety and depression in her later years. Many want to know why; why did she turn away from not just society, but even her own family? She was not a woman who never had connection, after all. She had friends, love interests, acquaintances, and family who she deeply loved. Why did she choose to hide away from them in that room at the top of the stairs?

Most of the theories surround various deaths in Dickinson's life, those of her nephew, her father, and her mother—and if not deaths, then departures of both friends and love interests. Others point to a depression she didn't have the tools to combat. I wonder if part of what stuns people is the fact that she did not actually depart. She did not walk away. She did not escape. She hunkered down in her house. She took to her room with a fierce devotion; she protected it like a child. She encased herself in her space; she protected herself with herself.

When Dickinson died, her sister-in-law and friend, Susan Gilbert, wrote about two kinds of mourning. She not only mourned her death but also mourned "afresh that she screened herself from close acquaintance." And isn't that always the way when one chooses to depart? We can't help but wonder why they went if they were so loved and loved, too: why couldn't they bear a certain closeness?

***

During that summer, I was having a harder and harder time bearing closeness from anyone but B. Friends—both those who knew what I was going through and those who did not—tried to reach out and often, I deflected. I didn't want to talk to them because when I did, a feeling would surface in my chest, one I could neither breathe through nor get rid of; during that time, I felt I was carrying a ghost inside me. It lurked in between my belly button and my chest. When I was asked, "but what are you going to do?" it would grow. When I said, "I don't know," it would hold its own breath, thereby constricting mine. "I can't talk about it." "I don't want to talk about it." These were the words I used, but they did not do justice to the ghost. Perhaps I should have been more clear that the body I was carrying was no longer my own. The me that had once had my hair, my legs, my teeth, and my toes was not the same me any longer.

***

Usually, when you see a vulture, it is eating carrion in the middle of the road. Often, it does not seem phased by the passing cars. It takes its time to grab the sinew, guts, and muscles, to eat its way to the bone.

***

Throughout the tour, B. and I tried hard not to laugh. At points, Steve's intensity was hard to take seriously. When we got to the part where Steve started dissecting Dickinson's poetry using wooden blocks, we smiled. Here was one of the greatest poet's works being played with as one would play with toys. It felt like a joke falling flat, except that it was of course not a joke. One can't blame them for trying, but one can't help but feel a bit sad, not simply for Dickinson but for those whose only introduction to her work will be this: a mostly untouchable house, with one playroom full of em-dashes.

Perhaps we didn't simply laugh because it was funny but because we were uncomfortable. At that point, we hadn't spent ample amounts of time alone together, at least not out in "the real world." Our graduate program was a bit like camp, and even then, we didn't identify our feelings for one another until the semester before we'd almost graduated, so there wasn't much of "the real world" to navigate. Most of our interactions were on email or the phone. When we did talk, we used most of our time belaboring our situation: ever changing and ever the same. We couldn't stop being in one another's lives, hard as we tried, and yet we were attached to the lives we had still, and so we were stuck, or so we believed ourselves to be, encased in a new house of our own making, full of things we could not do.

***

The tour concluded with a second house tour. At the end of our time in Dickinson's house, we were led next door to her brother Austin's house, called The Evergreens. It was there that we learned about the years-long affair Austin had with Mabel Loomis Todd, who would go on to make Dickinson famous, likely to Dickinson's dismay—not simply because Dickinson did not choose to publish much of her work but also because the affair disgusted her. On the tour, we were told that Dickinson was so uncomfortable with the affair, she stopped visiting the house entirely.

Austin's house was messier. Darker. One or two paintings were on the floor resting against the wall. The thread was giving way on the couches, and the paint was ballooning on the ceilings. One could imagine feet on the floorboards and wine spilled on the carpet. One could see children with cookie crumbs falling out of their mouths and perhaps a dog or two running up and down the stairs. Lives had been lived there. The house had accepted its decay while just yards away, Dickinson's house was seeped in preservation, not necessarily of the dynamism of her work but of her desire to close herself off to the world. I felt myself in both states at once: accepting of the inevitability of loss and full of a desire to ward it off.

***

The vulture does not pause before its food, considering whether or not to eat.

***

When the tour was over, we went to get food. Our clothes were still wet from the rain, and the bar's AC was turned high. Shivering, we joked about Steve and his stiffness. We talked about the vulture. Like two people who had just shared a long trip together, we went back through the entire day, reminiscing on the experience. When we walked back toward the cars, the sky was turning dark, and we made our way into his car. Behind us, Dickinson's house stood tall. I could see it in the rearview mirror as we reached for one another's bodies over the center console and rain hit the windshield.

***

In my car, a few feet ahead, a mouse was avoiding a mousetrap. I'd seen the mouse a few days earlier. It had popped up on the floor below the passenger seat. I thought I'd seen something out of the corner of my eye, so when it appeared, I was somewhat relieved. But I was also terrified, and I slammed on the breaks and pulled over on the side of a country road. I got out of the car and opened all the doors. I turned the radio up, figuring it would be scared and run out of the car and into the woods. I said to myself that it was more afraid of me—and distant voices on the radio—than I was of it, but I didn't really believe it.

I'd put traps all around the car, but the mouse avoided them, and when I drove up to Dickinson's house, the mouse reappeared. This time, it was more bold. It crawled up and onto the seat. To stay calm, I told myself it wouldn't crawl over and onto me, as if I had any idea about what this creature would do. Eventually, it scurried away.

When I got to Dickinson's house, B. and I put a mousetrap in the bag with bits of scone I'd bought. I didn't want to kill the mouse. I also never wanted to see it again. But I was only twenty minutes into my car ride home when I saw it, hopping over the seats in the back, mocking me with its presence, with its real, boundless life.

# A Collection of Losses

On Miami Beach, people look for lost items. They walk with metal detectors searching for rings, bracelets, and buckles, moving the device from one side to the next, down and back along the shore, skimming the edges of the sand. Rarely do they find anything worth very much, and yet they have all kinds of equipment attached to their bodies to pursue what others have lost.

A friend of mine lost his wedding ring so many times he bought himself one for fifteen dollars. He didn't understand how anyone kept their ring; it seemed so easy to lose while washing dishes or taking out the trash.

When I got engaged, I was worried about losing my ring. Some people said to keep it on—to never take it off—and others said to take it off when I swam or showered. The rule seemed to be that if I was going to be in water, near water, or around water, I should protect it at all costs.

Even though I am no longer married, I worry about the whereabouts of my wedding ring. Given that I moved it from my house where I was married to an apartment where I was not and then into another house with a different partner, it seems logical that I'd lose it. Or misplace it. The ring is still where it was when I took it off: in the red jewelry box where a bracelet from my great grandmother lives. The bracelet is the one M. used to pull diamonds from when he created the engagement ring; now, they are in there together—the bracelet, the engagement ring, and my wedding ring.

During the initial Covid lockdown, I heard a story about a hairdresser who paid house calls to her clients, particularly those with grey hair. She said many of them panicked when they were told they couldn't go to the salon because she was the only one who knew they were going grey. No one in their families knew they'd lost their color, that the strands had gone from one shade to the next.

There's a person I keep referring to as lost because she lashes out, and when people lash out, they seem lost to me. Perhaps this is the stereotype of being lost, perhaps some people are more calm in their being lost—they sit with it and don't look for the next exercise class, acupuncture treatment, colonic or exfoliant. I am not sure if looking for any of those things means you are lost; if it does, then we are all lost.

Growing up, I was known as the messy kid. I was the one whose clothes were always on the floor, the one who always lost her stuff. If I was only more organized, I heard people say, I wouldn't lose things. My messiness was a deficit. It was not OK to be messy, to not know where items were. It was not good to lose things.

I live with a seven-year-old who is messier than I think I ever was. I never had many toys or dolls, and all of my make-believe places were those that my sister created for me. I never built lands and worlds and fantastical locations where all of my stuffed animals could be friends. I never even understood what a stuffed animal was for, but I knew that it was important to have a favorite one and to prize it above all else. I decided on a big fluffy rabbit and made a big deal about how he was my most precious stuffed animal, but I never really had an emotional attachment to him, even though I made everyone believe I did.

B.'s daughter, V., knows the whereabouts of every animal, toy, doll, scrap of paper, marker, and hair tie. She will locate them out of nowhere and panic when she sees that they are missing. Her mess sometimes delights me, but most of the time, I see it as a problem. I have voices in my head telling me it is important to put everything away, keep things clean, never leave anything out lest you lose it, and I sometimes feel myself wanting to get angry or yell at her for her mess.

A part of me is also envious. Neither of her parents force her to part with her items, nor do they make a huge deal out of keeping those items in tidy places. She's asked to put some clothes and toys away, but she's never told that she is wrong for making the mess she made. I am both jealous of this and jealous of the mess itself because her mess is her imagination laid bare, almost crafted, and I wonder if my mess had been that way—less clothes, more toys, less tossing, more placing—mine might have been respected, too.

I had it ingrained in me from an early age that I was someone who lost things, so I was always anxious about losing things. One time, driving home from Boston, I convinced myself I'd left my backpack at the house I'd been staying in because I didn't see it in the back seat. About half an hour into the drive, I decided I had to go back to get it. I was convinced I'd left it behind. When I arrived at the house, I discovered the backpack in the trunk. Just where I'd put it.

I thought I lost all of my earrings during the two years I was leaving my home in D.C. I kept them in a bag that had belonged to my grandmother. The bag is needle pointed and covered in cats, and when my aunt gave it to me after my grandmother died, I did not ask questions. I put all my favorite earrings inside. I used that bag to carry the earrings with me across the country. I also took it on a trip to Ireland and to Rome. I was on those trips because I'd lost something and could not recapture it. Months later, I lost the bag, and I had no idea where it was. A year later, my sister said she found it. It was in her house in Dublin, tucked into her bookshelf.

During the years I lost my ability to be home, I was corresponding with a poet about an essay. With each letter, she'd send a treasure: a collage, a cut out of a newspaper, a paint swatch. One of them was a postcard, and over top of it, she taped a thin piece of paper that said "write. write. write." I wish I'd framed it the minute she sent it to me, but instead, I lost it in a book I left on an airplane while traveling somewhere I don't remember. We met a few times that year. Once, we met at a lake near the school where I'd met B., and when she discovered what I was going through— separating from my husband, joining the person I loved and his children— she said now was not the time to talk about sentences.

Everything V. touches moves somewhere else in the house. She builds worlds of tiny toys on window ledges and the floor. For a long while, she was creating little sleeping nooks for all the stuffed animals wherever she could find a "blanket." The animals ended up inside masks and socks and pillow cases and dish towels.

The other night, she thought she lost her favorite blanket. We were making the bed for a sleepover party, and we pulled all the blankets off. As we were remaking the bed, she wanted her blanket to go on first. But she didn't see it, and she started throwing all the blankets around, whipping them through the room. When she nearly knocked over a water glass and her dollhouse, I told her to calm down. "It has to be here," I said, "it has to be," and it was. When we found it, she became quiet and resumed making the bed as if nothing had happened at all.

When I fell in love with B., I felt like I'd lost a part of myself that I understood. This part was my ghost, the one always haunting me with its presence, saying: "remember, remember, remember."

After college, a friend sent me a sketch. In the sketch, a button is flying off a shoe. During the end of my marriage, I wanted to get a tattoo of the string and the button flying. I never got the tattoo. The only tattoo I have is a house that a child might draw, on my right shoulder.

It took me over two years after falling in love with B. to finally take off my engagement and wedding rings, the ones I never lost, never lose. The red box is kept in the drawer with my socks and underwear.

"Laura, how do you spell the word lost?" V. asked me the other day. L. O. S. T. She was making "missing" signs for her lost stuffed animals to put around the house even though she knew exactly where they were.

"I've already lost all the way up to third grade," a friend said. "Do I have to remove fourth grade too, to let these new memories in?" I was visiting her just weeks after her sister died. People would say she lost her sister, or they would say how sorry they were for the loss of her sister. I'm not sure those words suffice. She didn't lose her; her sister didn't wander off. She died.

If I search my photos for "lost," nothing pops up. The phone can call up an image for the words "winter," "grass," "fog," and "trees," but it cannot find images of "loss."

The other night at dinner, B. looked out the window and saw the dog who always walks by our house. He pointed it out to V., and she looked at the dog, and said he must be a stray. He didn't have a collar. She said maybe he walks by here on his way home. "Strays always make a home," she said.

V. recently brought out a foam football for a different dog to play with. The dog was her aunt's dog, and she was feisty and slightly aggressive. But V. was convinced the dog might like the football, or be at least willing to play catch. Instead, the dog ripped it into pieces, and they went all over the lawn. We decided to take a walk with the dog down the path. V. started to collect wildflowers. As we made our way back, she said we needed to have a memorial service for the football. She pulled off the petals, one by one, and then covered the dirt road with the small white pieces. She thanked the ball for the joy it brought us; the ball was still strewn across the lawn, yards away. We didn't bury the object. We buried its memory.

When I met the poet at the lake, she'd just had Lasik eye surgery. She was debating whether to go into the lake without her goggles, just to see what it was like. Ultimately, she decided against it. The new sight did not take away the memory of the sight she'd never quite had.

The hardest part about leaving a marriage is the idea that you are choosing loss. Loss is always terrible, but when it is an accident, it feels less harmful somehow, or perhaps it's easier to let go? I'd lived my whole life never having to break up with anyone or anything. Or, perhaps it's better to say: never having chosen to do so. I had always been loyal, committed, and reliable, which is not to say selfless. In a way, staying attached seemed easier, almost more powerful than letting things go. People had left me, but I'd never chosen to leave a person, and I used that as a badge of honor, a way to counteract the reality of loss, or at least make it somebody else's fault. I now realize this was futile, and in some ways, hurtful. The art of leaving is a muscle one must build, and if you don't, the ability to move forward, to leave, to choose to lose, will atrophy.

One of my aunts always has new adages, often about letting go. One summer, she repeated, "let go and let God." This summer, she is saying, "snip snip" as a way to cut off what is upsetting or distressing. "Snip snip," she told me as she was taking down decorations after my brother's wedding. "Snip snip," she said, as she took down the tule, the flowers, and the wallpaper. "Snip snip" to the unwanted thought, the gossip, the presumptions about other people, she said. "Hear something about you that someone else said? Snip snip!"

The same week we buried the pieces of the football without burying the pieces of the football, I heard a story about loss that made me laugh. I was with B.'s mother, who was telling me about a bike ride she'd just been on with another couple. The man in the couple had been married to one of her best friends, Susan, and she'd died recently and unexpectedly. The husband had moved on quickly, and reconnected with an old girlfriend, who they were biking with. The girlfriend was not used to biking, and she kept falling. At one point, she fell badly enough that the two men had to go back and get the car. As the two women sat on the bench, the one recovering, the other trying to comfort, B.'s mom said, "It must have been Susan."

Deer leave their babies for the first day of their lives. After the baby is born, the mother places the newborn on the ground and goes off to recover, gathering food and nutrients, knowing that no predators will find the tiny fawn because the babies have no scent.

I learned this about deer because a friend found a fawn on the edge of the golf course. She thought the baby was abandoned. She assumed it was lost. She called around, only to find out that this leaving was part of the plan.

When I learned this about deer and their babies, I thought it was a beautiful concept. What an act of faith to leave your baby while you care for yourself. What an act of love, I thought. Then I learned from my brother that while the baby deer are protected from most predators, they are not protected from human errors; sometimes, farmers will kill them while cutting their fields. This fact does not mean that the concept has no weight, but I can't deny that it loses something—it is hard to think of the act as beautiful without thinking about the ways in which it can be so instantly, so quickly destroyed.

Some animals mourn their losses. Or perhaps it's more accurate to say most do, but we are aware of the movements of elephants, giraffes, ducks, apes, and cats, and the ways in which they grieve. It isn't simply that they mourn the lost animal, but they also care for one another. There is documentation of fifteen dolphins slowing down to travel alongside a mother carrying her dead calf. Twenty-seven giraffes were captured holding a vigil for one dead baby. Elephants are known to gather around the bones of their dead.

I grew up in a family where death is discussed and acknowledged long after the fact. In most cases, when a family member dies, we do not gather immediately. We make calls, and when we cry, we cry mostly on our own. Then, months later, there is a memorial service we often call a "celebration of life." It is a performance, as much as it is a coming together, with the focus on life rather than death.

When I was starting the process of separating from M. and joining in a new life with B., the photographs of my M. were still up in my mother's house. It didn't bother me because it mirrored my own experience and the ways in which moving on was happening slowly. One of my aunts pulled me aside and asked me how I felt about the photographs and said that it must be hard for me to see them. She'd been divorced. In the conversation, I was uncomfortable, but afterwards, I realized that she was one of the only people who talked to me directly about what was happening in my life. This same aunt recently wrote me a note saying, "Please put all you know into words. Take your time."

Time is both the problem and the solution. It's the problem when you want to remember something you cannot; it's the solution when you want to lose the memories you thought you wanted.

B. and I started spending our summers together in the barn. The barn was built by my grandfather on my father's side, and it sits behind the house I grew up in. When my parents were divorced, my mother kept the house, and then she bought the barn. She did some renovations to it, but kept it mostly the same. In one room, there is tiling that was started and never finished.

When I moved most of my belongings out from my house in D.C., I brought them all into the barn. I moved the items in the winter, dropped them in the main room, and left them there. When B., his children, and I arrived, all the items were stacked in the main room, and I panicked and cried. I was not expecting to feel anything for the boxes; in a way, I'd nearly forgotten they were there. But when I encountered them—the photographs and mementos and postcards and letters from my relationship, from my marriage—I had to remember. Instead of getting rid of it all, I stuffed it into a closet upstairs. I asked my friends for guidance.

One of my friends told me to watch the Chris Marker film, *Sans Soleil*. I tried, but my internet was spotty. The film kept stopping and pausing, but this part played all the way through—

*The woman he loved died last year and he drowned himself in work...like a madman. It seems he even made an important discovery in electronics. And then in the month of May he killed himself. They say he could not stand hearing the word 'Spring.'*

In the barn, next to my desk, I found a copy of a wedding invitation for my aunt's wedding, the one who had been divorced, the one who had asked me about mine. It was covered in dirt, and I took photograph after photograph of it, for reasons I don't totally know or understand.

When I moved to an apartment five blocks from the ocean, I liked to walk to the sea and take photographs of it. One night, I walked down and took as many shots as I could, and in the span of an hour, I lost my glasses and my keys. The glasses went first, and I wandered, looking for them. In that time, I continued to take photographs, getting close to the sand and bending down to capture the details. My keys must have fallen out then—while I was hunting for the other item I'd lost.

"You always lose things," a friend said to me, and she was right. I forget where I put my glasses daily; I rarely know exactly where to find my wallet. When she said it, I had just lost my Metrocard. It was in my wallet, but I couldn't find it. I frantically went through each pocket, as she went through the turnstile. After I found it, stuck to the back of the ATM card, she said, "I couldn't live like that. It would make me so anxious."

No one means to lose anything. One doesn't leave one's wallet at the restaurant on purpose or forget their friend's keys at the grocery store because they want to. Perhaps someone will lie that they lost something they never wanted to keep—an ugly painting, a useless vase—but rarely does anyone claim agency over what is lost. In fact, it's hard to even pinpoint how the loss happened: *I was distracted, I wasn't thinking, I was rushing.* Even then, you might be able to articulate why it happened, but you can't fully express how.

Whenever I tell people in the Northeast that I live in Miami, I am looked at with dismay. Do you think you'll stay? people ask, and when I say yes, they are even more confused. Climate change, they say, the rising water. They are not wrong that the water is rising in

Miami, but I am confused at their hubris: do they believe themselves protected from all the loss we've all endured and will endure?

I am often lost in my dreams. I am often meant to be somewhere at a certain time, but I can't find my keys. Or I am in a performance where I don't know the lines. Or I am about to get on a train and then feel so nauseous that I cannot. I am always inching towards something and then finding myself doubled back and retreating from the thing itself.

What I long for are the dreams where I am lost but content. It's only happened a few times, but there have been moments where I've been in places so beautiful, I am confounded. In one, I was in a huge river between mountains, and the water was bright and clear. I was swimming by myself, could swim for as long as I wanted, and I did not feel afraid. I so rarely have those dreams.

## Pathless: A Tale in Two Acts

Director's note:
In the throes of falling in love with someone outside of one's marriage, the first major life decision one might make is to leave one's marriage. I understand that. I get that. I really do. But that's not what this play is about. Instead, it's about a different route, one easier to name to friends and family, one in which I chose to leave my job and do what my family has always done in the face of change: drive.

I didn't take one, two, three, or even four road trips. I took over a dozen, each one crafted with essential elements to bring legitimacy to the need for a trip—a novel experience, a novel place, or an opportunity for a novel connection. I was free, and I would bask in that freedom, traveling during the week, coming up with trips on the fly, and visiting friends repeatedly (some might say aggressively), all to bask in the new version me that had nothing at all (nope, nothing, not a thing to do at all!), with the fact that I had fallen in love.

I was used to road trips because my family was big on them. When we moved from L.A. to Connecticut, we drove across the country, building a foundation of memories we'd return to for years. There was the time my father tried to "beat the storm," driving as quickly as he could with our bags on the top of the car, only for the rain to catch up a few miles in. There was the singing along to the *Les Miserables* tape over and over and over, belting out, "Do you hear the people sing?" There was the fighting over which cereal box we wanted. There was the need for winter coats in Montana that would carry us through our first winter in Connecticut. There was my brother's penchant for gambling in Reno and his daring run in the calf scramble at the rodeo. There was fighting over who sat in the back seat and faces of dejection when told we had to sit in the seat that faced the road we were leaving behind.

***

I have yet to finish any translation of *Don Quixote*, but the concept of an errant-knight, roaming the country on horseback, attempting to amend the ills and right the wrongs, comes to mind when I think of myself venturing out on the road, in search of something new each time. It wasn't that I believed myself to be any kind of a knight, but I did perceive the trips themselves as a way to sort through what I'd been wrestling with for over a year and a half: I'd fallen in love with someone else, and I couldn't figure out what to do about it.

When Don Quixote sets off on his adventures, he first has to polish and fix his broken armor. His helmet doesn't close, and he has to fashion a piece of board onto it for full protection. He's satisfied with himself, and even tests it out, slashing himself a few times with his sword to see what happens. Immediately, it falls apart. He has to rebuild it, and when he does, he uses it "as a helmet of the most perfect construction."

In these acts, I see myself in this moment, over and over again. I fabricated various armors and then lashed out at them; upon doing so, I would immediately see their flaws and start anew. The plan to travel with both of my parents to cities of their choosing was one such invention, the beginnings of which were imperfect from the start.

When I asked my parents to take trips with me, I was not asking them in an effort to help me better understand their marriage or my own. These trips were perhaps my initial tests of departure, but I was unaware of it at the time, deceiving myself enough to believe that it was solely an innocent request, not part of a larger desire to depart.

I believed I knew my parents' beginning, middle, and end. Theirs was the story of two people with a fierce passion for one another that had faded, not the one I was in, not the one I was living. And yet, I had to admit that theirs was not simply that either: theirs was also the story of an affair, one that caused an irreparable rupture. Could I, should I, have seen these trips as opportunities to pry, to ask, to seek counsel? Certainly. Did I? Absolutely not.

I was convinced I'd built an altogether different narrative than theirs. M. and I did not fall in love as they had; our relationship happened slowly. M. became the person I wanted to talk to, the person I wanted to be around, despite not knowing it fully, despite feeling like perhaps he was too kind for me, too nice, not enough of what I'd dated before. We'd flirt. Over the phone, over GChat, and eventually together in offices around the country, working on the Obama campaign. It was unexpected, welcome, and safe.

My family loved him because he was "not like anyone else in our family." Which was to say: practical, stable, and good.

What could I, then, learn from our family?

## Act I

I wondered often if affairs were hereditary, and when my father chose Miami, the place B. lived, I wondered if affairs were not just hereditary but karmic. As far as I knew, I was the only sibling to ever see the woman my father had an affair with. One day, she came to the house with their son, and as I pulled into the driveway, my father rushed her into the car, and they drove away. I was told never to tell anyone what I saw. I never did. But I blamed my father for putting me in the situation, and the image stayed with me: my brother in the back seat in his pajamas; her long, red hair; my father's hands pushing her towards the car.

Then, years later, there we were, sitting on the dock where he'd proposed to my mother, talking about a trip we could take together, and him suggesting Miami, the city where B. lived, all for the love of a favorite airport restaurant: "Need I say more than La Carretta?"

I stuttered. I blushed. I didn't know if we should go. It felt too easy, too simple, for my father to have chosen Miami out of nowhere. I knew he knew more than I gave him credit for, but did he actually know where B. lived? No. He couldn't have. Then why would he pick it? I tried to get him to think about other places, but he was set. I had not factored in the possibility that he might have picked Miami of all places, and as much as I wanted to go to Miami to be near B., I did not want to have to ask my father to never tell anyone what he'd seen, so I convinced him to break the trip up, to go to the Keys, to Hemingway's house, "You'll love that," I said, "you've always loved Hemingway!" He agreed.

***

What is hereditary: the affair or how you write about it?

***

Here's how my father went about writing about his: he did it in a few, quick pages leading up to his getting a job at Starbucks. Perhaps he dedicated four pages. Perhaps ten. I can't remember. All I know is he moved through it briefly to get to the story he wanted to tell: that of a man finding himself through his job at Starbucks. He wrote: He met a woman at the gym. They had a child. Then, he received a brain tumor diagnosis. Benign, but still a tumor. Then, the loss of a house. The loss of money. And then, a wander through the Upper East Side. Only to find himself at a Starbucks with a kind, generous woman named Crystal, who said, "Do you need a job?" Yes. He did. And that is what the book is about. It is not about the affair, but instead about the job at Starbucks. Crystal. His life after marriage. After the affair.

***

When I was a sophomore in high school, my father's mother died. I remember that was one of the reasons my father gave for his affair—that he was depressed after the loss of his mother.

I was depressed too, not just because I loved my grandmother but because I knew I didn't love life as much as her. I was in high school, getting mediocre grades, starting to smoke weed and take shots of Bacardi Limon at parties and having various, unfulfilling hookups with boys I obsessed over. My true loves were seniors who would soon be graduating, and in particular, I was in love with a friend, a girl named Zoe, who I wished I could become. She loved me too, in the way an older girl loves a younger one because they can help craft them into versions of themselves. Over time, I started to emulate her—dressing like her, and cutting my hair short like hers. I even made out with her friends.

I went down to the lake that summer after my grandmother had died, after Zoe and the seniors had graduated, and I jumped in. I swam to the middle, and turned over onto my back. I put my ears into the water. I stared at the sky. It was clear, and I was floating. I thought, in the way one forces oneself to think things, in the way one convinces oneself they must think: *I will enjoy this life while I get to live in it.*

During those years, my father underwent a physical transformation. He saw an image of two fried eggs and bacon on the cover of the *New York Times* magazine and followed the image to the article about the wonders of the Atkins diet. From that moment on, he was eating only protein and losing weight rapidly. I am not sure at what moment, or on what day, he met the woman at the gym with whom he had a child, but many years before the truth came out, he was able to separate his two lives to the extent that "being able" means keeping two lives afloat. But his body indicated change, signaled a shift; his breath smelled of meat, and he carried Listerine strips in his breast pockets, popping them like they were candy.

***

What no one tells you about these kinds of things—that is, transformations—is that they don't always have a beginning. When you're in what you think is shallow water, just touching the water's edge, barely even in, you're already in too deep.

***

In the year of traveling, I often wished there was a way my body could communicate the lengths it was going to deceive itself. I wanted the muscles to atrophy and to lose enough weight that people would have to ask after me. Or maybe it would be hair loss. Or bitten fingernails. Or an incessant picking at my face. I didn't want anyone to know why I was fooling myself, but I wanted them to see the toll of that fooling.

What I thought was the edge was a night when my whole body became undone. I had been a woman who was in a happy marriage. I owned a home, worked a stable job, and spent money on vacations; then, in the matter of days, without having so much as held B., I was a woman who wanted something so badly, I was ashamed.

***

"You are just like your father," a family friend told me. I was nineteen and sitting in his kitchen, hoping to make out with his son. I was in love with his son in the way that you can be in love with the outer edges of a person. I traced the edges off and on from ages twelve to age nineteen, and when my father's affair was announced, I decided that he was the only person I wanted to be near. I went to his house often. I wrote a story about a girl who couldn't decide on what jeans to wear because I could never decide on what jeans to wear. I often chatted with the other members of his family, those nearest to his edges that I could find. When his father told me that I was like my own father, I was talking about what I wanted to do with my life. I was still convinced that there was something I had not yet discovered about who I was meant to be. I did not, however, want to be my father. He was living alone, and working at Starbucks. He read books all day and ruined their bindings. He was not happy, I didn't then think.

A few days later, I went to the son's room, and I sat there, next to his drum set. His girlfriend was in the house, complaining about her new haircut. I waited. I forced tears to my eyes. When he found me, I was unable to speak. I wanted to say: choose me, but I looked at the rug under his bass drum and I had nothing to say. That day, I had chosen my ripped jeans. My knees jutted out. He said, "Why don't you come back downstairs?" I stayed still. He walked to the door opposite me and left.

***

When my father and I arrived in Miami, we got off the plane and went immediately to La Carretta. I thought we might figure out a way to get our bags first, but my father said, "No, no, no—this is what we are here for!" I was worried about the luggage but followed. Rice and beans and chicken covered our plates and hands. "It's as good as I remember," my father said.

I was anxious to get the baggage. I was anxious to get to the hotel. I was anxious to get to B. I ate beans and rice and shared in my father's delight. "Delicious!" I pretended like I could stay there all day.

The first part of the trip was my father's responsibility. We'd joked about renting a convertible, but when it actually pulled up, I was surprised. A bright yellow Camaro would be our trusty steed, and we were handed the keys and given very minimal instructions on how it worked. What seemed immediately clear was that there was no way to put the top down and put our bags in the trunk. So the bags went in the backseat, and there we went in the front, onwards to South Beach.

The hotel was the SLS: "What, nothing gets an actual name anymore?" my father said as we left our bright convertible with the valet. The hotel had a sequined bull's head in the main lobby, and the color scheme was pink, black, and white. In the bedrooms, there were mirrors over the beds.

***

After my father went to bed, I met B. at one of the many souvenir stores in the city. I was looking for a sun hat to take on our trip to the Keys. It was the first time I'd seen him in months, and I was nervous. He was too, and we didn't know what to do. Any encounter was full of the weight of every conversation, email, and exchange beforehand. Being in Miami felt surreal; in a way, it was a gifted time, and as so often happens with a surprising gift, we felt surprised and ashamed at our good fortune. What were the chances?

We didn't know that would be our first time together in the city where we now live. Perhaps we both did know, but we didn't treat the time that way; instead, we met one another with a stifled enthusiasm. If there is a way to be full of desire and express it gingerly, we did. We did not map out our future. We stayed trapped in the present: together with restrictions, in love with boundaries, trying to figure out a place to go that could fit our need for privacy and a decent beer. I projected my anxiety onto my father: "Let's not go too far away from the hotel in case he calls," I said, "but let's not be too close in case he ends up seeing us." I did not act like the adult I was because having that amount of agency created too much responsibility. It was easier to imagine there was someone out there whose judgement mattered more than my own, but it didn't necessarily make sense to place that onto my father, a person who had cloaked himself in lies for years. Wouldn't he be one of the only people who would actually understand?

We resisted the hotel for hours. When we finally gave in, we went up to the room together and nearly couldn't get on the bed. The mirror over us was not simply over-the-top and ridiculous but altogether too metaphorical; there was the universe again, telling us we could not hide from these bodies, we could not hide from ourselves.

***

My whole life my mother has said that my father is a bad driver. She was worried I would be one too—that I might get excited about a song on the radio or a story a friend was telling and crash. She said I was distracted, just as he was, and that it made her nervous. I later wondered: do bad drivers have affairs?

When we drove to the Keys, I drove. "Are you worried about my driving?" he asked, and I was. I had been my whole life and was certainly more worried now. He was in his late seventies, and the last time he'd driven me, we'd narrowly avoided both accidents and arrests. He could tell that I was keeping him from the wheel.

It was cloudy, but we were fearless. We trusted our Camaro even though we knew nothing about how it actually worked. We followed the family motto, "Beat the storm," despite the evidence that this had never been successful, despite the fact that the rain drops were starting to fall. Our bags were exposed in the back. We were exposed in the front. The rain kept coming, and my confidence grew. I saw there was a button to bring the folding roof up and over, and I pressed it, imagining the top would come up and over us. It didn't work out that way, or if it did, the experience of watching the top move up and over us as we sped on the highway was too terrifying. "No, no, no!" my father said, "leave it!" And I did.

***

My dad joked that I had a real knack for timing with these trips. Hurricane Irma had battered The Keys just a few weeks before, and in Las Vegas, where I was set to go next, there had been a mass shooting at a music festival. "How'd you plan this so well?" he laughed, as we drove through on the highway surrounded by piles of wood, palm fronds, plaster, and ripped billboards. In the natural landscape, there was erosion. Trees split. Sand pulled away. Of people, their items peppered the landscape: a recliner on the beach, shoes on the road, boats on their sides.

I remarked that the landscape didn't entirely look as I'd expected. I didn't know if it was because of the hurricane or because I had the wrong idea about the Keys. I'd never looked up the area or read about it. I simply had it in my head as a place that dealt in luxury, a place that cultivated some quaint, old-fashioned taste. When I mentioned that to my father, he started to laugh. "Oh no," he said, "the Keys are not that. It's the place for anyone to go and anything goes."

We were trying to get to Key West by sunset. My dad loved the idea of a whole town going abuzz for the sunset, and that is exactly what happens in Key West. Around dusk, people start to gather and walk towards Mallory square, the gathering place for the best view of the water and the sun.

***

When we arrived at our hotel—an old, colonial-style building with bungalows all around—we were given our keys and a flier about Fantasy Fest, a month-long celebration. Of what, we were not sure, but in reading the list of events, it seemed to be organized pregaming for Halloween. We'd arrived on Tutu Tuesday and were told there'd be all sorts of festivities to attend. We looked at one another, laughed, tucked the flier somewhere far away and headed to our rooms before our walk to the pier.

We saw the first group of revelers as we exited. They were wearing green wigs and neon tutus and running across a crosswalk with drinks in hand. We continued to walk down the main stretch and encountered more and more people in tulle skirts, body paint, and wigs. My father whispered under his breath, "The worst part is these people have day jobs," as we nearly walked into a topless woman handing out tickets for free drinks.

We arrived at the pier to a crowd surrounding a man performing a juggling act. My father wanted to steer clear, saying, "He's probably about my age" as he feigned a look of horror. We looked out over the water and onto the horizon. The sky was gray and flat. We could scarcely make out a thin, pink line cutting through. I attempted to take photographs as we waited. Perhaps it wasn't time? Eventually, my dad called it as the lights around the pier started to turn on. "Well, I think that might be it," he said.

In town, there were more and more people flocking to bars and taking shots in the streets. Sidewalks were awash in exposed skin, chest hair, and cleavage. I thought we'd try to get out as soon as possible, but my father said we had to go to Hemingway's bar and have at least one drink. He doesn't drink, so it was up to me to have the lone beer in the back corner of Sloppy Joe's Bar as we continued to avoid the crowds. I took one or two photographs, and in one, there's a middle-aged man in a pink leotard, placing an order at the bar, with hundreds of bras above his head.

***

In the morning, I took a run. I took photographs of what seemed to be on the verge of escape. A purple plant forcing its way through a break in the concrete; a pink pedal in a puddle, floating above a reflection of telephone wires; waves crashing behind caution tape. I wasn't simply interested in the escape, but what was put in place to try to prevent it.

When I made it back to my father, he had a ring of coffee around his lips and a huge Styrofoam cup. He'd somehow convinced the people at the coffee shop to give him two Cuban coffees in one container: a nearly heart-stopping amount of caffeine.

We discussed our plans. We decided we should go to Hemingway's house and then head back to Miami a day early. I like to think I let him make the decision—that my urge to return to be closer to B. was not overly apparent or obvious—but I cannot be sure. What I do know is that I quickly changed my tune on Fantasy Fest: what had been an unfortunate surprise now turned into a great excuse to get out and get back.

We arrived at Hemingway's house when it opened, and it was already humming with people. There was no line, and no instructions. We were the ones to have to track down a person and ask if there even was a house tour, and while we waited, we sat at some chairs in a garden, greeting the six-toed cats. One came over and started to crawl onto my dad's lap. "They think I'm Papi," he said, "even they are confused!"

Our tour guide had long, blonde hair and bangles on both her wrists. She wore a cowboy hat and had a scratchy voice. Her skin was tan and wrinkled, and she talked quickly. We walked with her through the house, hearing the stories many of us already knew about Hemingway's life in Key West. The cats were everywhere, and when we were in Hemingway's bedroom, listening to our tour guide talk about gatherings held at the house and fights that took place between Hemingway and his wife, a cat puked blood. There were murmurs amongst the group, quiet whispers of, "Do you see that?" until one person said, "Excuse me, I think the cat is sick." Her interruption was ignored. A small circle of pink had stained the lace bedspread, and we continued to walk outside.

***

In my father's book about his affair, he wrote about his father and his father's friends, among them people who knew Hemingway personally and spent time with him. In the book, he wrote about one of his more wild stories about meeting Hemingway. When he traveled to Europe, he was somehow given instructions on where to find Hemingway during the Running of the Bulls. When he found him, Hemingway suggested that my father do the run. He then did it, nearly killing himself.

He wrote about his father, but he did not write about his father's affairs. He left this information out, and I am not sure if he did so to protect his father or himself.

***

The tour ended, and my father told me about the details about Hemingway the tour guide had missed. He told me about his plane accident, his suicide, his son's suicide, his personality, and his fame. He asked me again if I'd read his book, and I reminded him that I'd only read *The Sun Also Rises*. In high school, we read it after reading Fitzgerald, and because one of my friends who I loved told me she admired his sentences full of space, I also admired the way the sentences left space.

On our way back to Miami, I drove. What my father had said about the drive had been right: It was the best part of going to Key West. It wasn't just the sea itself, stretching out on both sides towards the horizon, but what it bore: small islands, an old railroad, sailboats, and underneath, a landscape I'd never see.

## Act II

The night my mother and I decided to go to Las Vegas, we were sitting under the stars. We had gone to "Mexican Night" at a quaint New England house-turned-restaurant, and we were tipsy on margaritas. I said I'd never been to Vegas, and she said, "Me neither!" and we both started laughing. "I think we should do it," I said, and she somehow agreed: both of us baffled not just at the idea but the actuality of it.

***

Las Vegas roughly translates to "the meadows," a fact that is hard to understand if you've been to Las Vegas, now a thirsty desert. But Rafael Rivera referred to Las Vegas as "the meadows" in 1829 when artesian springs peppered the lush landscape. Before his naming, there were no meadows, but instead, and perhaps even harder to imagine, marshlands. Rivers ran through the earth; mammoths roamed across what is now a broken shell.

Las Vegas is no longer known for its meadows but instead other man-made attractions: pools, fountains, casinos, and hotels, all of which are relied on, in part, by a man-made dam.

***

They say when you are in love with someone you are not married to that you live a double life, but in truth, you live a fractured one. You are the scarecrow in *Wizard of Oz*, losing pieces of yourself, trying to tuck them in as they fall out. With each iteration, your undoing transforms you, only to be undone again.

***

Las Vegas made sense to us because it made no sense. There was no reason for us to go: no show, no event, no particular pull. It was just a place we'd never been in a landscape we didn't know, which was probably why my mother wanted to bookend the trip with a visit to Los Angeles—a place where we did know people, where we once had a home.

***

Los Angeles and Las Vegas are only the cities they are because of their dams. In Las Vegas, the Hoover Dam gives way to the famous water shows and dancing fountains. In Los Angeles, it is the Mulholland Dam and subsequent reservoirs that give way to the amusement park and sets.

At the start, the plan was for Los Angeles to have two dams: the St. Francis Dam and the Mulholland Dam. The dams rose up in the hills like monuments; the concrete was stacked, and the aqueducts were attached all the way from the Sierras to just outside what would become Los Angeles.

The St. Francis Dam did not go as planned. Months into the project, the engineers noticed that the St. Francis Dam was getting too full. As the months went on, pressure built and cracks formed. Then, piece by piece, the dam started to collapse, and the water escaped over farms, homes, markets, and towns. Hundreds of people were killed.

A few days after the flood, the site of the collapsed dam became a tourist destination. Those that never saw the dead had forgotten about them entirely. People flocked to the site.

***

I grew up in Los Angeles thinking it made sense to live in a place far away from where both of my parents had family. I knew pools more than lakes, palm trees more than pine.

We moved there for my father's job, but it was my mother who embedded herself in the community. She met neighbors, joined the bell choir, made connections with parents at the school, and by the time we left, had close friends, some of whom made us a quilt. The quilt still hangs in my mother's house, on the way to the attic, where much of my father's clothing, papers, photographs, and old advertising copy still lives.

***

When B. learned I'd grown up in L.A., he was astonished. He said he grew up loving Los Angeles for reasons not even he could name. He'd never been, but when he was young, he decided his favorite football team would be the Los Angeles Rams. He lived in western Pennsylvania, outside of Pittsburgh, in the town where his parents met and were married just out of high school. It was Los Angeles he sought; Los Angeles he rooted for.

***

A frontier is a place you've never been but want to go to for reasons you don't quite understand. Perhaps it's the wildness. Perhaps it's the unknown. Perhaps it's a desire for something you know you need but haven't yet found.

***

We were planning to take Rt. 15 the whole way from L.A. to Las Vegas, but there was an accident on the road, so we went through the Mojave National Preserve instead. My mother was nervous. She kept saying, *This is how we die*, as we went further into the desert without a gas station or a car in sight.

I wanted to stop and take photographs. I wanted to capture the formations in the land as they went on out of sight. I had never seen anything like it. The plateaus never seemed to end. The shadows from the clouds made the hills and trees look almost purple; the red of the earth mixed with the blue of the sky.

I convinced her to stop a few times so I could take photographs, but she rarely got out of the car. One of the only times she did was at a rest stop across from a closed and discarded post office. My mother's favorite photograph from that trip was one I took from the bathroom. I took the photo without being able to really see what was in the frame. I raised my arms up to grab what was in the small window above my head. In it, you can see an old railway, and it looks like a painting.

***

I was most afraid of telling my mother about what I was experiencing, not just because of the damage my father's affair had done, but because she was an avid reader and one of the smartest, if not the smartest, people I knew. Her knowledge of narratives made me feel naked. My story—the one where I meet B., fall in love outside of my marriage and can't wrangle myself back in—would be too obvious, too typical, and for that reason: avoidable.

Beyond that, I was not reading. There were numerous books I could be reading, books that would perhaps mirror my experience in some way, perhaps even offer up some guidance, perhaps even comfort me, but I could not let words in.

***

Leading up to the trip, people asked us, "Why Vegas?" My mother and I both love to travel, but we don't necessarily love to gamble.

"Why Vegas?"

Because we'd never been, we said, we wanted to see it.

***

In the process of always leaving but never really going, the act of self-deception was so acute that I could sometimes believe what I was experiencing was normal, or if not normal, at least endless.

But then, moments would arise, out of nowhere, and call me back to what was true—I was a wreck. Take this: six months before our trip, the live action version of *Beauty and the Beast* came out, and watching it, I cried so much I surprised myself.

Before it came out, I'd read numerous feminist think pieces on how terrible the storyline was for women. People were getting really worked up over it, despite the fact that it was just another part of the Disney machine we'd all seen, and, frankly, grown to love. *It's a movie about abuse,* people said. *It is a fairytale about Stockholm syndrome,* others wrote. *Not only does Belle endure abuse, but she grows to love her abuser.* I was ready to join groups crying out for its insidious story line and see the film for its numerous flaws, but instead, Belle walked onto the screen singing, "I want adventure in the great wide somewhere / I want it more than I can tell," and I wept. I wanted something more than I could stand, too.

We don't always choose our guides.

***

What Jung said about love is true: it dismembers you. But what he didn't say was how to live in a dismembered body when you've vowed to stay in another. I spent every day shattering, trying not to show my cracks.

***

My mother's favorite song is "Don't Fence Me In." Or perhaps it's more accurate to say our favorite song to get her to sing is "Don't Fence Me In." At parties, she can often be coerced into singing, "Give me land, lots of land under starry skies above / Don't fence me in!" She'll start solo, but inevitably others will join at the refrain and sing alongside her, nearly yelling: "Don't fence me in!"

I remember her singing it most often when we lived in Los Angeles. Perhaps it was my father that coaxed it out of her, or perhaps that was a time where she felt most free. I always thought she embodied the song, looking beautiful as she sang it, gathering up more and more people along with her as she repeated the words.

***

Desert means to "abandon in a way considered disloyal or treacherous." It also means a "dry, barren area of land, especially one covered with sand, that is characteristically desolate, waterless, and without vegetation." The noun and verb derive from Latin words meaning "something laid waste" and "to leave" or "forsake."

Many people left something to enter the desert. They went to a barren place, a place of waste, a place where what grows is not what we dictate, but what must grow instead: cacti, Joshua Trees, and yucca.

***

When my parents divorced, my mother did not leave. She stayed in the house, and she did not change its shape. Photographs moved and were replaced, but my father's presence remained. He had left, and yet the house did not show signs of abandonment. His decorated bathroom was still covered in frames with his handwriting behind the glass.

It would have been easier for her to toss his presence out. We are used to seeing this: women carrying their husband's items and throwing them to the curb. If they don't, we assume the woman is unable to move on with their life, treating their ex's items as sacred and precious. But my mother held a different truth, one she likely felt bound to for our sake; however terrible his actions, he was still ours.

It's only now, over twenty years later, that she's demanding some of his stuff be gone through and thrown away, and even then, she is not adamant about how quickly it happens or with what force. She wears his old bathrobe with his name embroidered under her left shoulder as she asks, "Do any of you want this?"

***

On the way to Vegas, my mother said the only person she'd known who spent any time in Las Vegas was her friend who needed to get a divorce in the eighties. At that time, you weren't allowed to file for a divorce unless you'd lived apart from your husband for over six months. Two weeks after legalizing gambling, Vegas legalized a speedier process for divorce; you could get divorced after just six weeks of living apart. Dude ranches where women could go to live separately from their husbands were built as a way to help women file for divorce more quickly.

The idea of divorce as a process one might want so much that a person would move away from friends and family to get it done in a speedy fashion was not something I understood. I was trying to slow everything down, so I could see the contours more clearly, and I believed that there might be a way I could.

***

My mother didn't calm down until the road changed from dirt to asphalt. We started to see rows and rows of solar panels, and we stopped at a gas station next to a hotel with a roller coaster in front. The gas station had a sculpture of a person with a headdress on top of, as if it was the gas station's mascot. I asked her what music she wanted to hear, and she requested the Grateful Dead. We listened to "American Beauty," and sang along, "Truckin,' got my chips cashed in..."

***

The sun was starting to set as we saw the city in the distance. Huge, bright billboards called us in. We pulled off our exit, and onto the Strip, barely able to take in the various people in the crowds: hikers in Patagonia gear, women covered in feathers, families with matching t-shirts, women in saris, men in pressed suits, and babies strapped to backs. My mother's nerves returned as we pulled up to the Bellagio behind a row of cars. There were people everywhere. Some gathering, some alone, some stumbling, some moving with determination and force.

What, exactly, were we doing here?

We made it to our rooms through throngs of people moving in and out of the casino. In every pocket of the Bellagio, there were small, complex relationships playing out—coworkers together on a retreat, families on their vacation, older retired couples, and the regulars, none of whom I would be able to pick out of a crowd. It wasn't clear who felt at home or who felt estranged.

***

That evening, we watched the Bellagio fountains dance. This, my mother loved. The water sashayed, twirled, and shot up into the sky along with the beat, and she was taken. "How do they do that?" she said, as water appeared as moving feet, arms, and legs.

***

My mom was happiest when we left Vegas to go back to Los Angeles. She took the wheel and said: "We are going the normal way this time."

As we drove, I turned on an episode of *This American Life*. One of the segments was a piece of fiction, titled "If Wishes Were Horses" by Amy Bonnaffons. In it, two women undergo physical transformations. One wants to become a mother; one wants to become a horse. The story charts the ways in which their bodies change and focuses on the permanence of the experience. At one point, the woman turning into the horse starts to doubt her decision: does she really want to go through with it? But it's already too late. She already has hoofs.

## Beginnings: A Series of Attempts

Perhaps it began with a decision.

I did not get married in the family veil. In fact, I did not know there was a family veil until after I was engaged, and even then, I did not completely understand what it meant to have a family veil at all. Even the way my mother asked the question—"Do you want to go see the family veil?"—was off-hand, as if it had always been there, as if I had always known it existed, if only I'd asked. We'd have to call cousin Sandy, and we'd have to find a time to go over to her house to help her grab it from the closet. This was also surprising. As far as I knew, cousin Sandy had never been married, and her house was not a house we popped into very often. But there were two truths about getting married that involved Sandy: one was that she held the family veil, and the other was that she was generous with beds, bathrooms, and the other houses she owned during the wedding weekend, offering them up to friends and family.

I'd look at the veil, but I was likely not going to wear it. I had few strong opinions about how I looked for the wedding (or at least carried myself as though this was true—often saying just how little I cared as I went through dresses in my bedroom, wishing I did actually look different, wishing I actually did appear a certain way), but I did know I wouldn't wear a veil, especially in front of my face. I didn't even want to wear makeup, hoping not to really appear any differently than I always did. That was marriage, after all, the full embrace of one another as we were. I didn't want anything to get in the way.

The veil had been in the family since the late 1800s and my great grandmother, grandmother, mother, aunts, and others had all worn it. On the front of the box were names and dates listed, many in pencil, precariously placed one after the other, bride after bride, generation after generation. We pulled it out of the box and held it up in front of a window. It was winter, and the light outside picked through the lace, highlighting its details.

***

Do you get along with your sister?
What is your favorite item to unload from the dishwasher?
When did you know you were an artist?
What did your room look like in your childhood home?
Who is your closest friend?
What sports did you play growing up?
When did you first fall in love?
Do you have a favorite root vegetable?
How do you handle the heat?
What did you have for dinner?

***

The first and only item I ever stole was a purple bracelet: opaque, glass beads around a thin, white string. Soon after, it broke, but I kept the beads and broken string with all my other jewelry for a long time.

I'd been in boarding school, and I was with friends who were stealing too. They'd done it before, and they didn't really feel guilty: "I mean, they are charging so much for these cheap sunglasses," they would say. Rich kids stealing from rich stores. When I put the bracelet in my pocket, I pressed it into my hand, moving the beads around one another, unable to let go.

That year, we were obsessed with sex because none of us had ever had it. Our art teacher asked us to create an art project around one word, and we chose sex. We put condoms all over the big red poster, with the letters S E X in the middle and giggled at our audacity.

We knew, at some point, our virginity was something we'd lose, but we didn't know just who would take it, and whether they would steal it or we'd give it away. One friend lost hers on an animal print rug in front of a fire, and we discussed how romantic that was, just like the romantic version of losing one's virginity we'd seen in *Dawson's Creek*, where Joey and Dawson have sex for the first time. We'd all decided that was making love, or something like love, and we vowed to have love be a part of our making, even though the idea of a vow, like the idea of sex, was foreign to us. What did it mean, exactly, to vow to love while you moved your body toward another, fumbling with sheets, clothes and underwear?

***

I took Latin in high school and mostly earned Cs. Perhaps I had a few Bs, and I know I had some Ds, but C was my steady result, announcing my mediocre, nay average, capabilities. For some reason, I thought it was a good idea to take the course for two years in a row despite realizing I did not have a gift for the language. I am sure part of that decision had to do with the boy I sat next to, wrote notes to, and sometimes found myself kissing on the weekends. I did not think I *like liked* him and did not want to date him, but I was into the kissing, and very into the passing of the notes and the fact that he also took Latin because it didn't quite make sense that he took Latin—he was a jock, and not, as far as I remember, a serious student. But I have a feeling he did better than me in the course, and he did better than me at finding other people to kiss who did *like* like him, and I was always jealous of the girls and of him for being able to do what I didn't feel I could: let myself be liked, let myself like.

The boy I liked never wanted to kiss me, and I liked him more for it.

***

For some, it starts with a confirmation.

When we moved to Norfolk, my grandmother wanted one of us to get confirmed in the Congregational church, and I was the target. I spent a year with a group of kids and a Sunday School teacher, going over pieces of the bible on the weekends and one night, having to go to a sleepover. I can't name a person who was in my group, and I can't even remember the name of the teacher, but I know that I didn't like him. He didn't seem to have a sense of boundaries. Or was it simply that he was odd and his oddness made me assume he didn't have a sense of boundaries? Mostly, I didn't want to get confirmed because I'd never been able to believe in the bible stories whether they be metaphorical or literal: was Jesus actually, and I mean actually, real? Clearly, he was not. But he was. OK, but then: virgin birth? Walking on the water? Miracles? Returning from the dead? None of that could be if he was actually real, right? Wrong! Or right? It didn't seem to matter. What mattered was that I did this for my grandmother. What mattered was that despite me having no recollection of the experience, I became a part of a church I rarely go to and don't feel much attachment towards.

I don't wish I was more religious, but I do wish I had faith.

***

B. taught me how to take a bath. I had been in a car accident, and I was in a hotel room trying to salvage the self-imposed writing residency I was no longer able to drive to. I said I hated baths. I didn't want to take a bath. B. said I should try. He said it would help. I said I'd read this article in *The New Yorker* about how women's relationship to baths revealed something about the patriarchy and perhaps that was why I always hated taking them, but the truth was that I'd just never been able to sit there long enough to reap the benefits. He said he'd talk to me, and we'd get through the time together.

As I ran the bath, we talked. He was alone over Thanksgiving break too. We were working on our writing. We were working on our thesis projects. We were working on imagining being together—talking throughout the days, finding one another as much as we could. He told me to place him down somewhere close. I put the phone on the toilet seat. He said to keep the water temperature just right. Don't let it get too hot, he said, and remember to put the Epsom Salts in first. The water was cloudy and warm. I took off my clothes, and went in.

***

Is the first kiss an ending or a beginning?

And if it's a beginning: which one is the beginning? And if it is an ending: which one ends it?

Is it the first, *first* kiss? The one I waited for, from the age I knew a kiss was something I'd never had to twelve, when it finally happened? Or is the beginning the absence of the kiss, the longing for it before it ever happened, imagining what it might be like, considering its contours?

I liked the experience more than the longing, but I can't deny that within the longing was also something I enjoyed.

***

The pufferfish carves the sand to attract its mate. Its fins create tiny hills at the bottom of the ocean as it moves in circles, placing a small circle in the center, and then another, and then another, around and around, building a space for a potential mate to lay her eggs. It's hard to imagine how beautiful this home could be, but to see it—the mounds and circles and the flurry of sand—is to understand something about the structures we build and what we build them for, which is to say: what we craft for another can hold a beauty we'd never create for ourselves.

***

My parents were engaged the day they met, and they married two months later. Growing up, the story held a kind of legendary lore covered in big, summer flowers and long, glimmering nights. They met at the lake during a party in August. My mother got into a pedalo down at Frog Beach and went across Tobey Pond to my aunt's party at Drumsna: "The Gill dock." Then, she met my father, and my father asked her to marry him that night. She didn't really believe him—she said, "If you are serious, meet me tomorrow at the fountain in town"—but she also said yes, too, at least enough to give him permission to announce the engagement to the entire party. It wasn't until a few years ago that I was told without asking just what it felt like when my parents walked back to the party, hand in hand, and announced their engagement. My aunt said, "Can you imagine? Such a shock!" Then, I did imagine. Mouths agape. Smiles stuck. Some tears. Confused clapping. It was all very sudden. All very impulsive. But wasn't that the Gill way?

***

I was applying to college while my father was carrying on a years-long affair. I didn't know these events were happening at the same time, and I don't know if my mother did either. What I do know is both my mother and I were on edge. I wanted to take a year off. I didn't want to put myself in a position to be disappointed. But I already was. Each of my friends had seemed to know what to do about the college process and had a vision for where they might go. Their visions did not include having received Cs in Latin class and a few B-s along the way in subjects they just couldn't "find the time for" because they were perhaps more focused on school than they were on flirting and friendship. Or was it that they were actually smarter, actually more equipped, and better than I was at school and therefore deserved an education much more?

On one college trip, my mother pulled the car over. She said she could not handle my attitude. Did I or did I not want to go to college? I had no idea. We'd already battled about what to wear. I told her that I wanted to wear whatever I wanted to all my college interviews, and she wouldn't have it. She didn't appreciate the confidence that I'd acquired, one in which I assumed everyone would form around me and my views and outfits—jeans, a t-shirt, and my hair askew—and not the other way around. I conceded and wore slacks and a billowy, blue shirt to my interviews, and I smiled as much as I could muster, feeling like I did when I was confirmed in the church without knowing if Jesus was actually a real person. I felt fraudulent and embarrassed.

***

After college, I worked at a mediocre coffee shop and learned about what we can, and cannot, save. More than a mediocre coffee shop, it was a middling deli, and each day, we unwrapped the prepared foods and then wrapped them again and placed them back in the refrigerator. I knew every item had to be cared for; the chicken salad needed to be mixed up and stuck in the refrigerator, covered and sealed; the fried eggplant could last one more day, only if no air was allowed in. But I never got the hang of the Saran Wrap. When it was time to put the items away, the plastic would wrinkle and shift in my hands, and there was never enough.

***

My left foot was taped the day of my wedding. In most pictures, you can barely see the thick white strip on the side of my foot. In the one where I'm walking in with my father, though, it appears:

the frayed edges and ribbed lines of the bandage. My sister secured it moments before I walked down the aisle. We were in a room below the venue. The World Cup played as my brother and father ate the leftovers from the sandwich I'd been told to eat. My sister pressed my foot with one hand, and with the other, pushed the tape on and up, just as the physical therapist had taught her. Soon after, she went with my brother to take her place, and my father and I sat patiently in front of a table topped with empty champagne glasses, bobby pins, and crackers.

***

What excited my great-great-grandfather about electricity was the idea of being able to light up the countryside: "All the advantages of the city will soon be possible on the farm without having to put up with city life. . . Heretofore we have been compelling electricity to take us to the city. Hereafter we shall simply touch a button and have it take the city out to us." Norfolk, a town just few hours from New York, was the place his daughter and son-in-law would take their electricity; there, they didn't simply want to light the countryside up but instead save its forests, using their money to establish what we now jokingly refer to as a commune, a place where aunts, uncles, cousins—first, second, third, once-removed, twice-removed, and step—live.

When the family moved from L.A. to Norfolk, we moved in with my mother's parents while my parents fixed up my father's parents' house. We'd move a year later; decades later, we'd find out it was full of trapped memories we'd either gotten rid of or transformed, causing rifts and arguments amongst the family I'd never been aware of. Coolwater is one such house, but when we moved into Coolwater, it was still my grandparents' house; my grandfather was suffering from Alzheimer's, and my grandmother was often frustrated, mostly cross. What I didn't know then was that she was also grieving: each day, a new loss; each day, a sudden realization of my grandfather's deterioration. But with her, the grief was agitation and sometimes anger, and unfortunately, those were pieces of her she already carried, and so the grief served as a heightening to the scariest parts of her, and we were there for the bloom.

She made her rules known. She did not want to see towels on the floor, hair unbrushed, or clothes scattered all over the room. It followed that when she saw the towels crumpled on the bed, the socks scattered across the floor, she yelled. When my grandfather misplaced his tie or his toothbrush, she yelled even more because she didn't want disorder, and she didn't appreciate chaos, at least not in others' lives.

But she was equal parts loving and helpful, too. The drove us to the bus stop in the mornings. She took us to TJ Maxx to shop for back-to-school clothes. She cooked us meals. She bought us new towels despite the fact that we didn't know how to treat them. She found great deals on underwear. And she was excited by, and enamored with, the new choir director in church, who had a children's choir she wanted me to join. She took me to see them at the library, and I sat right in front, where my eyes landed on a boy, singing and smiling, with dark hair, blue eyes, and dimples on both cheeks. I was in.

For my audition, I sang "Edelweiss," or, rather, I belted it out in a way that was not so much singing but a kind of guttural calling out, a kind of desperate plea. I see myself standing at the piano, breathing deeply and opening my mouth as the choir director nearly laughs. I think he was somewhat surprised to hear this young girl in an oversized t-shirt sing one of the most famous songs written for an adult, male voice, and not just sing it, but give it her all.

***

I have a tattoo of a house on my right shoulder. I tell people it doesn't mean anything. I tell them it's not the beginning of anything. When asked about the tattoo, I respond: "I just liked the image!" because the summer before I got it, I did like the image: I was constantly drawing houses on scraps of paper, on letters to friends, in the backs of books. I was working at a summer camp where I lived in a tent built on a platform and used milk crates for drawers and bed frames. I'd never been much of a camper, but I enjoyed the set up. I liked being able to sleep outside without sleeping on the ground, and I liked living in an open space with men and women—a house without rooms.

When I got the tattoo, I said I wanted it to look like "the kind a kid might draw," and that is exactly the house I have.

My first idea for a tattoo was an infinity symbol. I'm glad I didn't get it, but I know why I liked it, and I know why I was drawn to its circular shapes connecting in a kind of wave. An infinity symbol is the opposite of a house, in a way, and yet, I think when I got the house I saw it as a symbol of infinity, as a never-ending home I'd always carry with me. Now, I see how it cannot be what it is not: my house is not an infinity symbol but a house—a fragile, breaking shifting, thing.

***

In a college course, we were asked to write essays about our bodies. Afterwards, our professor was surprised at the ways in which we had separated ourselves from our bodies. For instance, she said, people wrote about an illness as if it wasn't a part of them. And yet, she noted, *you are all your bodies*.

My piece was a letter to my body. I wrote it in the second person. It was an apologetic letter. I worried that I'd damaged my body when I let it be used by a man who said: "We cannot kiss, but we can have one another's bodies." At the camp that summer, that is what we did. In a creek. In a tent. In the car. I told my body, "I am sorry I let you be used." But the worst part wasn't the using. The worst part was the pleasure in the face of the using. And perhaps even worse: the desire for more.

***

Most of the essays in my graduate school thesis were written before I had turned towards B. They are disembodied; in fact, they rarely mention the body. They concern themselves with matters of the mind, focusing on concepts like marriage, feminism, family, and fear. Then, the semester when B. and I were writing one another constantly, sometimes holding back, sometimes holding on, stopping when we'd gone too far, returning when we couldn't resist anymore, I wrote what I now see as a beginning in an essay's ending:

*I don't know how to not separate myself from my body, and when I think about my body, I think of it as an abandoned house. I see vines moving through open windows. I see broken bricks and chipping paint. There are flowers growing in an empty fireplace. There is mold gathered under the sink. There are memories hidden in piano keys. If you peer under the stairs, you may find grass. With each collapse, something rises: a nail, a screw, a thought.*

***

I started writing this book at my first and only artist residency when I thought it was a book about traveling around the country, going from author's home to author's home. The same poet who told me that affairs were not hereditary had told me to keep it simple: just write about the houses. Include some photographs. Keep it observational. Write from a distance.

The residency was in a big house in a suburban part of Illinois. I imagined I would spend all day working and reading and luxuriating in my experience as an author, as an artist, as a writer. Instead, I spent the days as I'd spent so many days that year—slightly hungover, confused about where to begin, and on the hunt for distractions. Each night, I drank too many beers with people that were never going to amount to lifelong friends. Somehow, they were able to get up in the morning and create. The poet boasted about how many books he read per day while drinking whiskey and sneaking cigarettes. The dancer cut through air after nights of cheap white wine. The novelist entered the despair he needed to wrestle his book from himself while he "borrowed" my beer from the refrigerator, always with the promise of getting me back. One of the people who was there to party was a woman who talked about just how much she'd figured out: about marriage, about being a parent, about being a writer. She said she and her husband had discovered the beauty of an open relationship—how it really was the way forward for all marriages. A year later, she published pointed reflections on her divorce on Twitter, gaining followers by the day.

***

In the beginning, B. told me I had a good eye. He told me this as we shared a blanket, willing the night to continue. Instagram was a couple of years old, and I had been using it often, posting all kinds of photographs and not thinking twice. I liked what I liked, and mostly what I liked were pictures of friends. Sometimes, I posted a leaf holding onto a branch or the reflections of trees on a creek or an old corner store. He said, "You are better than some of the art students I teach." I didn't know what an aperture was. I'd never been into a dark room and seen an image take shape. "None of that matters," he said.

***

Before we were married, M. and I took a trip to Norway. Halfway through, I told him he had to spend a day without his camera. I was annoyed with all the stopping and starting, I said. I wanted him to experience the city with me and not be focused on the photographs. He complied. We spent the day together, and he did not stop and start, but he also likely lost something in the process. I allowed myself to have my phone. I allowed myself to take photographs. But he was not allowed to carry around his camera bag, consider different lenses, point and shoot.

To write about that day brings up a feeling of cruelty, perhaps because I know what happened later, which was not just that the camera I forbid that day was eventually stolen from our house but that when he went to buy a new one, he bought one he wanted us to share because it seemed like I was becoming interested in photography. He wanted to support that interest; he wanted me to have all the tools I needed to thrive.

I'd go on to use our camera on my trips to author's homes. I'd use it to capture images I wanted B. to see. To begin with cruelty does not seem right, but there is no way to begin without it, to not admit that within each start was a spark that eventually burned a house down.

# Southern Loop

When I told a friend I was going to drive through the south to visit authors' houses on my way to a friend's wedding in St. Louis, she said, "You'll love taking photos in the South." When I asked why, she said "It just really fits in with your aesthetic: abandoned things, things falling apart." Lonely, lost things. Things teetering on the edge. I suddenly felt obvious to myself—me, another woman on the verge of divorce, running toward what is broken to understand what can, and can't, be saved.

And yet the plan (which was what exactly?) seemed as good as any: to go to more authors' houses, write about the experience, photograph it too, and spend time on the open road figuring out what to do with my one precious life (indeed!). Who would I pick? Authors I loved? (maybe!) Authors I knew? (kind of!). It didn't so much matter. I had now been to many authors' homes, and I could continue on with my year of aimless (that's what *you* say!) searching. With a wedding in St. Louis as my final destination (weddings always make for a great ending), I would travel alone and build myself into the person who was strong enough to actually reckon with their life.

***

If you've read *Don Quixote*, you know that after the first attempt at departure, he finds himself back home—beaten down, turned around, and stuck in second gear. A priest and a barber try to cure his delusions and pin him down for good. They take all the books about knighthood and chivalry and decide to burn them; without the stories to lead him forward, he will have no choice but to come to his senses. But like so many attempts at control, this one fails. The priest and barber don't take responsibility for burning the books in the library. They tell him an enchanter came with a dragon and took the books because he held a grudge, which sends him off on his next adventure to find revenge, and the story continues in the pages of stops and starts of the wayward knight.

***

I had been asked to do a reading at the wedding in St. Louis, which was surprising to me, but that year, not entirely rare. All around, friends were getting married, and there were often requests for participation. For one friend's ceremony, I opted out of the reading and asked if I could do a speech at the party instead. I was honored to be included, but I also felt sheepish about being linked so directly with the moment they said their vows. What did I know about marriage? Who was I to speak on commitment?

What I did know is there were a few authors' houses along the route: Margaret Mitchell's, the Fitzgeralds' and William Faulkner's. I'd go to those houses, wander around, take photographs, consider my predicament, and *voila*! The book would come and all of this would make sense. But the truth was that I'd already tried this tactic. Weeks before, I'd gone to a Poe museum in Richmond and Thomas Wolfe's house in North Carolina with no new sense of what I was doing and nothing to show for it. The words didn't hit the page in a fury. Most of what I was writing was written to B., in emails signed with emojis and my signature: LCG. I'd returned home in my same body, with my same thoughts, considering the same question: how does one leave a home?

***

In most of the media portrayals of women leaving their husbands, there is a sense of unbridled freedom, nearly manic delight. So often women are leaving men who were abusive, cruel, or violent. Their journey beyond home is one of ecstasy. They are free, and in that freedom, they do whatever they want.

I was not any of those women. I was stuck between the backstage and the stage itself, trapped in a curtain of my own making.

***

I was nervous driving. Instead of taking my hair down, opening the windows, and singing loudly, I didn't entirely want to be on the road. I hated when a car would appear and chart my exact path, turning at the same light, stopping at the same stop sign, even pulling into the same gas station. I hated getting out of the car even more than I hated driving it. I'd get out to pump gas and feel naked. No one watched me or everyone watched me; it didn't matter. I always felt exposed.

***

The first house M. and I ever lived in was a friend's parent's house in St. Louis. After Philadelphia, M. got a job on the campaign in Missouri, and he invited me to come. Surprising even myself, I said yes. His job was in the headquarters, and I took a job as an organizer, knocking doors all over suburbia. We lived together in the furnished basement and spent our days and nights working to elect Barack Obama.

We fell in love in that basement. We'd host friends and eat take out and drink beer. At night, we would both often be working, sitting side by side on bar stools. After working, we'd sit outside, share a cigarette, and go over our days.

I was often criticizing everything about the campaign, and in particular, felt frustrated with the numbers—the exact part of the campaign M. worked on. I didn't understand why so much emphasis was placed on how many doors we knocked and how many volunteers we recruited: *what about the quality?* I wondered. M. was patient and understanding. He was also exacting and experienced; he knew that my emotions around knocking doors and making phone calls were mostly insignificant to whether we would win. It simply had to get done. I was attracted to his confidence. He never wavered, never complained, never once appeared exhausted. I loved him for his consistency and drive.

We moved into this basement together before most of my friends and any of my family met him. Some people asked for photographs, and I remember a friend asking for one of him, and instead, I sent her one of both of us. In it, we are wearing white shirts and smiling the smiles of two love birds: the silly kind, the goofy kind, the almost blurry kind, the we-are-giggling-so-hard-we-can-barely-take-this-picture kind.

I was both in love and aware of the pockets between us, the spaces we could not access in one another. We were not entirely opposites, but we held onto worlds entirely our own. This was something I valued, something I knew was good to have in a relationship. The often-espoused yin-yang. We needed each other.

***

Years later, as everything felt like it was crumbling, it felt easy to point to those differences and blame them for what became the dissolution of our relationship, but every time I did, I knew it was an oversimplification. The problem with trying to explain anything is that an explanation is just a story, and you can tell a story any way you want.

***

The summer B. and I were on the blanket and made our first rule was the summer I fell and scraped my knees while running. I was in D.C., and I was distracted. I was making my way back down the hill from the Basilica on North Capitol street. To my left was the giant graveyard M. and I had walked through a year before, on our way to a friend's party. To my right was the road that led to the Capital.

On my run, I was thinking about B. and whether he'd written back or whether he would. I carried my phone with me, holding it tight. I was feeling full of energy, full of life. These were the days where it all seemed possible—the ones in which I could think about B. all day but not leave the comfort of my routine.

I felt good running. I felt my body under myself and trusted it. The downhill propelled me, and I gathered speed. Then, I hit my toe on the edge of the curb and fell, landing almost perfectly on both of my knee caps. I was upset and embarrassed but also somewhat relieved. The stop meant that I could now check my phone. I could see if B. wrote back. I could even get him an email before arriving at the house. I no longer had to wait.

I wrote to him that I hurt myself, and he wrote back immediately. Sometimes this happened—our emails would become like text messages, both of us there on the other end—and so I walked and typed as the blood bubbled on my knees.

Over time, the wounds turned from raw and scraped to red and circular, staying visible for over two years.

***

My first stop was in Athens, Georgia, where my cousin was finishing her veterinary degree. I decided to stay there for the night before visiting Margaret Mitchell's house in Atlanta the next day. My cousin and her husband had a new puppy, one that looked almost identical to their other dog who they'd discovered was dying of cancer. Once she learned the dog was dying, my cousin scoured the internet for a dog that looked as similar to the other dog as possible. I was surprised at how logical and matter-of-fact she was when she said that because one dog was going, she knew she'd need another. It wasn't that she wasn't sad about the other dog dying nor that she thought they'd be the same, but the fact that they looked alike would be a comfort.

I never asked if it worked, if when the older dog died, she knew she felt a different, perhaps less palpable grief, because a dog so alike her in look and feel sat beside her in a younger, healthier body. I suppose I don't even know what "working" might mean. Perhaps it wasn't actually about replacing the dog she'd lost, but acknowledging, before she even lost it, that it would soon be gone.

She told me to be careful driving to Atlanta, saying that Atlanta drivers were the worst she'd ever seen. She also told me to avoid rush hour. The next morning, I got up early and made my way to a coffee shop to wait out the traffic. I parked overlooking a valley. Behind it were mountains. There was fog covering them, and the sun was just starting to appear. Soon after, the cover would disappear, but I didn't wait around long enough to see what appeared in its wake.

***

Margaret Mitchell's house museum is in the city, but she only lived there for a short time and famously hated it, referring to it as "the dump." She didn't like the city, she didn't like the apartment, and most of all, she didn't like being in close proximity to all the people. Despite her distaste, she wrote *Gone with the Wind* there, and so a house museum was created in her name. A house but not a home.

***

My first understanding about the body as a set of unpredictable, often breakable parts was when my elbows would dislocate. I only remember it happening once, on a trampoline, when someone grabbed my arm, but apparently it happened quite a few times, and my mother would often repeat, "Laura's elbows can dislocate!" whenever I'd attempt a new activity.

My first actual break was on a family vacation on an island in the St. Lawrence seaway. I broke my wrist flying off the back of a large, orange chair when, one afternoon, someone realized the chair could be used as a kind of slingshot and that us kids could be used as projectiles. It was fun at the start. We'd sit on one side, and a large man would jump on the other, and off we'd fly into the arms of other adults. But something happened when I went flying the second or third time. Immediately, I screamed.

We got on a boat to a clinic where they gave me a splint and an ace bandage. It was dusk, and the water was choppy. We bounced along, and with each bounce, I winced in pain. That night, I remember waking up every two hours, asking for relief.

***

The entrance to Margaret Mitchell's apartment is a souvenir shop, mostly full of posters, magnets, keychains, and coasters with scenes from the *Gone with the Wind* movie. The main event is not the book but the interpretation of the book in film. Vivian Lee and Clark Gable are on shot glasses, towels, and postcards.

I'd never, and have never read, *Gone with the Wind*. I thought I might read it on the trip, as a way to sync meaning with what I was doing, but I decided against it. I was foolish, lost, and only interested in forward motion. I had seen the film version of *Gone with the Wind*, and one image stood out: Vivian Lee in her blue dress, walking through the dusty town, as everything she knows is ravaged.

***

As I drove through the South, a national debate was happening about whether or not to tear down monuments. People were demanding that statues honoring Confederate soldiers be removed. In many cities, there were protests and public expressions of disgust. The past, and the presentation of it, was being actively questioned, and the country was in divisive and violent debates about it.

Politically, I aligned myself with those who wanted to tear down the monuments. The images of groups of people covering the statues in graffiti and knocking them down were moving. But a part of me felt dissonance towards the act: does tearing down our past actually remove it? Or does it start to fester, start to hide?

***

I often caught myself going through old photographs, searching for answers to what had happened to me and M. I'd scroll back through my Instagram account or photo albums, hunting for times when I felt like my whole self and wondering if that self was still me.

It wasn't just me that did it; the phone itself had an algorithm to create the memories for me. I had already gotten off Facebook to protect myself from the "five years ago today" photo albums it started to create, but suddenly, the iPhone started to do it, too, showing me over and over again where I had been just a year or two years before. It felt aggressive, and the only way to combat it was to continue to take photographs—to add and add and add more images, so that new images would overtake the old ones, if not erase them.

***

The country has more house memorials than any other. We are interested in the ways famous people lived. The house memorials are mostly for white authors and artists, and they are mostly for houses built in the 1800s and 1900s. Theirs is the history the country is the most interested in preserving, and preserving in a particular way, with a haze of nostalgia and romance, rarely acknowledging the realities.

In ways, I connected with the houses: they were being asked to maintain something that no longer existed. In other ways, I had no relationship to them: a part of me wanted my past to run off without me and leave me behind.

***

Before leaving town, I went to a Greek restaurant, and sat on the sidewalk. I was in the middle of a downtown Margaret Mitchell would have disliked—full of people of varied backgrounds, living and working next to one another, taking their lunch breaks with coworkers, running errands, and going about their day. I was somewhat envious. I wished I had somewhere to be. I wanted a punch card, an office, and a coworker who would notice my absence. I had no idea what I was doing, or why I was there. No one was asking me to do this project and no one might ever know I did it.

***

When M. and I were first in Missouri, he tried to teach me how to drive stick. We were on flat roads, and he gave me the instructions I'd heard before: go slowly off the clutch, stay calm, don't panic. I tried getting into first about three times before calling it quits. It was never going to happen, and I got into the passenger side, breathing quickly and asking for him to take over.

Over the course of our relationship, it became clear that M. was the driver. I got used to him driving us back and forth from D.C. to Connecticut and wherever else we wanted to go. Over time, I started to grow more and more intimidated with driving; when I would drive, I would feel unsteady, particularly around bridges and tunnels. If I didn't know when they might end, I'd panic.

***

That year, I was often asked by family, friends, and even acquaintances: "What are you doing? Where are you going?" And sometimes they'd answer their own question, "You are everywhere these days!"

I was everywhere. I was also nowhere. I was in hotel receipts and suitcases packed and unpacked and dinners alone and interactions with strangers. In Portland, Maine, months before, I'd taken myself out to a fancy Japanese meal and tried to avoid talking to the stranger who asked me what I did. When I said I was formerly a teacher, and then went on to explain I was also a writer, he interrupted my answer with: *No, no. Don't tell me what you really do. Tell me what makes you tick, what you live for.*

I was living for horoscopes that never seemed to come quickly enough and never said what I wanted them to say: *This is the month in which you will know exactly what to do and you will do it without hesitation.*

***

I was hesitating because sometimes the memories would overwhelm me. Sometimes all I could see were mornings in bed and coffee being brought to my bedside. All I could remember were decisions about what breakfast bagel to eat and whether to walk to grab it. I saw shoes everywhere. Near the couch, the bed, and the door. I saw those shoes and the shoes made me cry because the shoes meant that we were trying to hold the house together. We were still going in and out, holding dinner parties and hosting friends, making food for one another and talking about our days.

Or maybe it's more accurate to say that the house was trying to hold us together. It was the place where our objects went, and it held them there, as if to say: this was real.

***

When M. and I left St. Louis and drove to D.C, we got in one of our first fights. We were driving separate cars, but we'd been following one another the entire way. Our cars were in lockstep. Then, close to D.C., we hit traffic, and his car went ahead. I lost sight of it, and I missed the turn off the highway. I was angry he hadn't waited, frustrated he had left me to fend for myself. He was baffled at my frustration. I had the address, he said. I knew where to go.

***

I was barely reading, but when I did read, I read books from the past, my favorite being *Middlemarch*. Even though I can barely recount any of the character's storylines aside from Dorothea's, and in particular, her attraction, and eventual engagement to Will Ladislaw, that storyline was enough for me. I had fallen in love with someone outside of my marriage, someone who was not like Will Ladislaw, but perhaps made me feel as he made Dorothea feel: wholly different in ways that were as terrifying as they were undeniable.

***

The first time I talked to B. inside the house in D.C., we created a new rule. We had planned to have a talk about our writing, thinking that being collaborators and peers was our best bet for staying in our lives and holding them together. We used FaceTime, and we didn't talk much about writing. The pull was so intense that he called me an hour later and said we could never FaceTime again.

Rule number two.

***

I booked a room at a Super 8 in Montgomery. I'd never stayed at a Super 8 before, and I had forgotten they were housed around chain stores and strip malls. I was slightly disappointed, perhaps more at myself than anyone because I was actually surprised. When I arrived, no one was at the front desk. I was yet again surprised, and yet again frustrated at my surprise: what was I expecting? I took myself to the bathroom, and wires were coming out of the hole in the ceiling. When I came back, I rang the bell at the desk. A man came and sat down at the computer and asked for my name. I can't remember if he said hello. He looked me up in the system and said no, I was not booked at this Super 8. I checked my phone. He looked and said, "Oh, that's the other Super 8 across town."

I decided it was all for a reason. I had wanted to see the Memorial for Peace and Justice, and I'd have to pass it on my way to the other Super 8. And this other Super 8? It was going to be clean and welcoming and close to downtown Montgomery, where there would be cute restaurants and places to wander. It was going to be quaint and comforting. A perfect place to rest my head.

But the National Memorial for Peace and Justice was closed for repairs when I arrived, so I got out of my car and walked around its huge green lawn that lifted up and over Montgomery. I could see the big steel columns hanging in the distance. I knew they hung in memory of Black men and women lynched and killed, and I discovered, in plaque around the outside, that the columns on the ground were waiting for different counties across the country to pick them up and take back to the place where those men and women were lynched. The memorial itself was very much alive.

The only places I'd previously seen preserved for their beauty were plantation homes. Peppered throughout the South, one can encounter them on main roads or back roads, sometimes established and sometimes less so, but nevertheless often cared for and attended to. Usually, there are placards with information about the family who lived there and a sign letting you know the times for visiting. Their big columns, porches, and windows stand as a remnant of the old South, or of a particular side of the old South. Though they often make a note about the Civil War, they never directly say: on this land, there were slaves.

The only other people I saw around the memorial were security guards, Black men driving golf carts around the perimeter. One told me to be safe and another asked where I was from. Then another asked what I thought of the memorial, and I said it was beautiful even though that didn't really make sense—it was beautiful but it wasn't *just* beautiful—and he turned to me and said, "It really is, isn't it?"

I drove to the other Super 8 through an area full of boarded up shops and houses on the verge of collapse. There were people walking into the street and sitting on porches in a place that felt entirely forgotten. When I made it, I didn't get out of the car. There were no other cars in the parking lot, and all I could see was a Burger King, a Wendy's, and a Sunoco. I looked for another hotel.

***

When M. and I were together, my desire for comfort was sometimes a point of contention. He enjoyed hiking, camping, and being outdoors. But even when he wasn't out in nature or on a trip, he was rarely itching to be anywhere he was not. I'd often tell people he was *good at life*. He could sit in front of a computer working for hours, then stand near a grill in ninety-degree heat, cooking up a meal for a large group before he passed out beers and whiskey and stayed up late chatting, ready to do it all over again.

***

I woke up to rain and quiet in downtown Montgomery. It felt apt that it should be raining on the day I would visit the Fitzgerald house. My favorite part of *The Great Gatsby* has always been the part where Gatsby bolts out into the rain when Daisy comes to Nick's house. He has been waiting so long, thinking his lost love might never show and then, when she arrives under "dripping bare lilac trees," he rushes out and walks back in, his hands in his pockets, "standing in a puddle of water."

When I arrived, there was a tent out front, which also felt appropriate: the aftermath of a party, a party Gatsby may have had. I walked through the rain to the entrance, and the sign said the house was closed for maintenance. They were sorry for the inconvenience.

***

I walked around the outside of the house. I photographed a bright green hose in the grass and a black plastic bag filled with sand. I tried to capture the rain falling fast through the gutters. I put my lens right up to the big magnolia tree and zoomed in on the droplet falling from the white petal. I didn't know what I wanted to grab hold of, so I took in whatever I could, hoping that at some point it would reveal itself to me.

***

My next stop was Oxford, Mississippi. All I knew about Mississippi was how to spell it, and the fact that Faulkner had lived there. Of his house, I knew it had a name—Rowan Oak—and I knew people who had been to visit. One friend said her visit to Rowan Oak devastated her. It was there that she realized what it meant to be a great writer, and what it meant was having hired help. It wasn't his house, but the small house behind his house—the shack, essentially, where his Black servant lived—that upset her the most. She had loved Faulkner in high school. She had loved his ability to dive into the psychology of his characters and play with form. She had also admired his range; he wrote about people and lives unlike his own. But she hadn't imagined that he'd lived with people all around him, serving him and attending to his every need.

It was because of her that I wanted to love Faulkner in high school as much as she had, even though I barely understood the books. What I knew was that the characters were strange, confusing and lost, and what I could feel when I was reading was just that: a feeling. I did not have a great understanding of the work, even if I wanted to, even if I thought I did.

***

The roads to Oxford were mostly two-lane highways. There were abandoned cars on the side of the road, billboards saying *Jesus Saves* yards away from ads for strip clubs. In the bathrooms, there were vending machines for sex toys, vibrators, and condoms. Aisles were dedicated to cheap bibles and dangling crosses.

At first, I thought the juxtaposition created a dissonance, but then I realized that perhaps the two went hand in hand—can you be saved if you haven't sinned in the first place?

***

Before we ever read Faulkner, we read Hawthrone's *The Scarlet Letter* and discussed adultery. I don't remember much about the book except for the first scene where Hester Prynne walks out of prison with the "A" embroidered on her chest. When I became a teacher, I used that scene to discuss point of view and imagery. I didn't have my students read the entire book, but I wanted them to see the beauty in the description of Hester Prynne as she walks out of the prison: "Never had Hester Prynne appeared more lady-like... than as she issued from the prison... that Scarlet Letter, so fantastically embroidered and illuminated upon her bosom... had the effect of a spell, taking her out of the ordinary relations with humanity, and enclosing her in a sphere by herself."

***

As I drove, I sought books and Ted Talks and podcasts and advice columns about affairs and their meaning. If I could not read much fiction, I could listen to people share their knowledge. Most of what I heard centered on how to stay with one's partner after having had an affair. The overarching message about affairs was that one should avoid them, but if one couldn't, then one needed to figure out what it was saying about one's current relationship. Likely, what the affair was telling you was that you'd reached stagnation, and you needed to work to change it up and go back to the love you had at the beginning.

No one ever spoke of an affair leading to a new relationship, one that was healthy or worked. Perhaps it was rare. Perhaps it was the reality that most people were having affairs to either blow up their lives or infuse their lives with something new. Perhaps there was also a fear of the unexpected and sudden.

After a friend of mine in D.C. found out about how my feelings towards B. had led to my relationship falling apart, he said, "Oh, well, I would never put myself in a situation to feel that way."

***

Oxford was quaint and charming. I was immediately grateful for what felt like solid infrastructure and a churning, lively community, and realized quickly that what I was feeling more than anything was wealth and whiteness. When I went to grab a bite to eat in my hotel, the room was filled with prospective Ole Miss parents. Many of the women had straight blond hair and many of the men had broad shoulders under tailored suits. They were drinking and laughing together, getting to know one another before sending their child away to what was likely many of their alma maters.

I got a tip from the bartender about where to get the best barbecue in town and then promptly ignored it. I went to a bar with a porch where I sat, watching and listening to people milling about. At one point, I saw two prospective students kiss and hug with an intensity I was nearly embarrassed to witness. Had they come there together from the same high school? Or did they just meet during this orientation? They did not cry, but instead looked at one another with a kind of knowing: they would see one another in the fall, and until then, hoped nothing would change.

***

I was close enough to walk to Faulkner's house in the morning, and I woke up in time to get there as it opened. But somehow, I got lost on my way. It was the kind of lost I had experienced before, the kind where you are exactly where you are meant to be—the map says you are right there—but you can't find what you are looking for. The map indicated I was at Rowan Oak, but in front of me all I saw was a driveway into a two-door garage. Most people would turn around and go elsewhere. I walked into what was clearly a private driveway, determined that the small blue dot on Google would not lead me wrong.

***

I didn't know Rowan Oak was a made up, mythical tree. There are Rowans, and there are Oaks, but a Rowan Oak is a Faulkner creation. Rowans don't even grow in the South. They rely on cold winters, and they need the chill to flourish. Oaks are almost the complete opposite—they could pretty much grow anywhere in the northern hemisphere, and they do well in the South, growing huge branches that reach out like light rays, covering the ground.

***

I eventually made it to the house. Down a dirt road, through a row of cedars, the huge white columns stood perfectly at attention. I wanted to discover my own version of Faulkner, but my friend's experience was ever present in mine. I could only find evidence of his having used the people around him to support his work and being so bullish in his passions as to scratch one of his stories into his studio wall, for everyone to see. And perhaps I only say bullish because of what was written on a plaque about his wife's desire for an air conditioner and his refusal to allow her to have one; in that anecdote, I see a kind of aggressiveness I was unaware of before. But I was not devastated, necessarily, at this new picture of an artist whose work I did admire; instead, I was slightly relieved.

***

I arrived in St. Louis the next day. The first night, I stayed with my friend's parents who had put myself and M. up during the Obama Campaign eight years before. They had moved into the city and out of the house we'd lived in together, and they were kind enough to take me out to dinner and take me in before I went to the group house where I stayed for the wedding weekend.

For the wedding in St. Louis, I chose the poem that was read at Obama's first inauguration: "Praise Song for the Day." I was friends with the couple because of the campaign, so it felt appropriate to read something that resonated with that part of our lives. In the poem, Elizabeth Alexander takes us through the hustle and bustle of the everyday: "Someone is stitching up a hem, darning a hole in a uniform, patching a tire, repairing the things in need of repair." She then goes on to talk about how many have "died for this day" so that we can enjoy the mundane, the normal, the routine. She then asks, "What if the mightiest word is love?"

***

I drove back from St. Louis through Ohio and Pennsylvania. I saw no more authors' houses, but I did end up in a town memorializing Jim Thorpe, a Native American football star. I arrived late to a hotel in an old, 19th century inn, and was grateful that the bar was still open.

When I woke up the next day, the town was covered in fog. I wandered through it, driving up and out of town on a steep hill, going further into the cloud. I stopped on a two-lane road to take photographs of the green and the gray. I gathered pictures of the telephone wires popping through the white gauze, and I was not in a rush to go home.

## Adaptations

When B. found us all a place to live, I wondered if I should keep the apartment on the beach. It made no sense at the time, but it makes sense to me now that what I was holding onto was not entirely the apartment, but our life as a new couple, one in which we gathered household items, cooked first meals for one another, and shared space.

The apartment did not fit the kids. They came there a few times, but only for short stints. I remember cooking V. macaroni and cheese as she sat on the kitchen counter, which was also the dining room table and a living room shelf. I don't ever remember being there with A., but I know he came at least once, on a trip to the beach, to shower and change and then leave promptly.

When B. found the house we all now live in, it was covered in grease, cockroaches, and dust. The second he bought it, he tore through it, removing tiles, cutting through ceilings, and redoing the bathroom. Each room has been torn apart, put back together, and sometimes ripped apart again. There have been days when my whole body shook with the sound of a drill making its way through the floor.

***

In the first year of us moving in together, *The New Yorker* marked our house as "undeliverable." When we watched footage from one of our security cameras capturing our mailbox falling off, it wasn't a surprise. The mailbox didn't just drop to the ground; it tipped back, as if it was fainting, as if it had given up. The mailbox, then a gaping mouth on the lawn, was too undignified for *The New Yorker*. But how did it know?

I was annoyed by the "undeliverable" designation. I wanted *The New Yorker* back. Weeks went by. I sent emails. I called. I missed the magazine. I begrudgingly read it online until one day that, too, was taken from me. A pop up exclaimed I was not a "subscriber." I went back into bank statements, emails, and confirmations. I was a subscriber! I am a subscriber!

***

When I first moved in, the children were five and eleven, and they immediately gravitated towards the *New Yorker*s. Every week, we would look at the cartoon contest in the back. I thought the contest would only interest the older of the two, but both of them started to love the ritual. "Is the new *New Yorker* here yet?" they would ask when they came in the door. Or, upon seeing it, exclaim: "a new *New Yorker*!"

***

Growing up, *New Yorker*s were piled on the kitchen table, backs of toilets and next to the TV. Even though my grandfather was a writer for *The New Yorker*, it never felt like that was the reason we had the magazine. I never looked for his name in the pages nor asked him about what was written. For me, the magazine was a pleasure because of its design. I covered my wall in *New Yorker* covers and made collages out of the pages. I had no idea that the writing meant anything beyond what it was useful to me for cutting out, pasting, and occasionally reading.

My grandfather who wrote for *The New Yorker* was my father's father, but I rarely saw my father reading *The New Yorker*. Instead, the magazine was something my mother read and continues to read. She leaves them near the bathtub and across the kitchen table. She recently said she was going to bring "all her *New Yorkers*" on her next trip to see me. Knowing that they are everywhere in her house, I wondered what that meant: three, five, ten?

***

For half of the week, I live with two children who are not my own. Since I started to live with them, I've learned there is a whole lexicon devoted to families like ours, which many like to call "blended." Within the lexicon are terms like "transition days," "bio mom," and "insider/outsider." These terms both do and don't give the experience a narrative that makes sense; on the one hand, they help to define a role that can sometimes feel unexplainable; on the other hand, they can serve to alienate you even more. There's a reason you don't see Hallmark cards for "alloparents," "bonus moms" and "second dads."

***

One day, V. made her own magazine styled after *The New Yorker*. On each page, there were mini articles and drawings. In the back, she put a caption contest. The cartoon involved a woman with a vase. I can't remember what else was in the drawing, but I know the vase was as tall as the woman.

***

When we lost access to the magazine, I became antsy that *The New Yorker* might never come. I was worried they'd forgotten about my need for the magazine, which I now see was a need not just for the magazine, but for how it connected me to the kids. The magazine gave us a way to communicate without communicating. So much of all of our lives had changed, but for a while, *The New Yorker* kept coming, with a consistency we all appreciated.

I started to hope that all the *New Yorker*s that had been held away would just arrive in a pile at my door, tied together with a bow.

***

Before moving to Miami, before falling in love with B., I planted my desires for change on a desire to move to New York. I'd lived in D.C. for eight years where I thought I was stuck. This was not the case: M. often said we could leave, but he wanted to know why we were leaving. He wanted a plan. It was hard for me to explain why I didn't want to be in D.C. after years of living there and building a life. I had close friends who were like family, a house, favorite coffee shops, and bars and restaurants where I was a regular. The life we built was a life full of abundance. Each spring, the dogwood in front of our house brought new, pink flowers; each fall, we hosted Thanksgiving, filled with friends and family and their families; each winter, there were snow days, and we would go sledding in Malcolm X park, and then find ourselves in a friend's house eating and drinking together. My friends were changing the country, and I worked at a school with students who would eventually do the same.

***

Now, I live close to an old hotel called *The New Yorker* hotel, a hotel on Route One, the route that leads right to New York. The hotel is in a neighborhood where there are many hotels and motels that appear stuck in the 1950s. Their exteriors are in the art deco style people have come to associate with Miami, and they pop up along Biscayne Boulevard: Selina Gold Dust, The Vagabond, Shalimar, and Saturn Motel.

***

When my mother came to visit with all her *New Yorker*s, we went on an airboat tour in the Everglades. We cut through sawgrass and mangroves and small islands of brush and alligators. Even the parts in Miami that look like a city do not look like a city because they are on land so close to the water that you can feel that you are nearly drowning. One might think that because New York is an island, one could have this feeling, but I never have. When I am in New York, I never think of the water, but of buildings and people. In Miami, I think about the varied, wild species surrounding us.

***

When my mom left to go back to Connecticut, she left a *New Yorker* on the bed. It was one I already had, which irked me. I wanted the past issues, the ones I'd never received when the New Yorkers had stalled their delivery. The one she left was one I'd already tucked behind the toilet in the magazine rack, never to be touched again because there was already a new one in front of it, opened to an Ann Patchett essay I was excited about.

The essay was about her three fathers and how they influenced her life. I wanted to read about these second and third dads and how they'd been able to guide her in some way. These were the stories I started looking for, stories I'd never looked for before. Before I left M. and moved to Miami, I wanted stories about writers who were domestic; writers with partners and children, who lived lives amongst the tried-and-true structures happily and with success. The more time I spent living with the kids in our new home, the more I wanted to hear about people whose lives did not fit easily into that model, lives that were not only upended but rebuilt.

***

During the start of the pandemic, V. would help me to make collages for friends and family. Like me, she liked the smaller illustrations on the pages of *The New Yorker* and the ways in which they worked with the bigger, brighter pictures she also liked to include.

As we built our cards with cut out pieces and tape, I kept a pile of *New Yorker*s above my desk. Over time, all of them were demolished, but still, we'd pull them down and go through each one over and over, just to make sure we didn't miss a gem.

***

When I first moved to Miami, I stayed in Airbnbs around the city and had no bearings. I knew one person who was from Miami and she kindly let me know whenever she was visiting her parents. I then ran into one old friend from college who took me to his favorite Cuban grocery store where we ate big thick pieces of white bread with melted butter on top. He had also been divorced, and we discussed losing one life and entering into another. In those years, I was always hoping to find some kind of fairy godmother, and in a way, I thought I'd perhaps found it in him, even though after that day, we never shared a meal again.

***

Many writers go to die in the pages of the *New Yorker.* Often, an author has learned they are dying or feels old enough that they might die, and *The New Yorker* publishes their work and reflections, sometimes even posthumously.

My grandfather died on his way to work at *The New Yorker*. My father mythologizes this part of his part of the story, saying he died alive: striving for the next great sentence, hunting for the next great word. My grandfather acknowledged his age often, spoke of death, too, but was not interested in leaving behind some kind of afterword to his life. He believed his legacy was already in the magazine, in his books. He didn't need to explain anything to anyone. What he loved, admired, criticized, and despised was all there for anyone to read. We are left with just the work.

When people ask me what type of writing I do, I often shrug. I write nonfiction, I say, but not the real kind. I write about me, myself, and I, I say, as their faces go blank. I am not always sure what they think, but I know what some do: why?

***

Both kids enjoy *The New Yorker*, but it is V. who covets it, which is surprising because she is not a kid who spends her days reading. But there have been days where I've left *The New Yorker* lying on the couch, only to find it with her, in her room. One day, she took it to the beach. She started reading it in the foyer, then walked out the door with it in her hands. She got into the car, still with the magazine in front of her face.

***

Susan Orlean first published her essay about John Laroche, the "orchid thief," in *The New Yorker* in 1995. The article then became a book which then became the movie, *Adaptation*, in which Meryl Streep plays her as she follows Laroche into the Everglades. Laroche is a person of passion: the narrow, focused kind that leads a person to go to great lengths, even risking their life, in the pursuit of what they love.

In the article, she writes about the desire for orchids that Laroche has, and she seems to get his drive for these plants who can "have adapted to almost every environment on earth."

***

We have a few orchids. One bloomed this year. It was over four years old and had not bloomed since the first time I bought it when I was at a residency in Illinois, working on the book I was always working on.

That summer was the summer M. and I officially separated, just days after our four-year anniversary. No one there knew. He sent me lilies and a card. I didn't send anything to him. When we spoke, I told him I couldn't continue to pretend I could ever come home. After two years of flailing, I was not able to get back to the self that committed for life, forever, through it all.

I had yet to know where I would be living or when I would be living there. I was a year into traveling around both aimlessly and purposefully, knowing I had to end my marriage and not knowing how. The orchid was small with purple flowers. I brought it with me from Illinois to Vermont, where I met B. for the first time since I was separated. The orchid stayed in Vermont until I came back to get it, and then it traveled with me to Connecticut, which would become my home as I went from there to D.C. to Miami and back again.

Finally, I moved to Miami, along with the orchid. It lived with me in the apartment. It never bloomed, but the leaves stayed shiny and green. Then, it moved in with me to the house. The flowers bloomed in our second year of living together as a family, four years after I bought it.

***

My grandfather had affairs, but he never left his family, if to leave means moving your body out of the house into another. I have learned through the pain still stuck in my throat that you can leave in many ways without leaving, but the fact remains that my grandparents had a fiftieth wedding anniversary party I attended, sang at, and remember fondly.

***

One day, I arrived home, and *The New Yorker* was in the bathtub, its pages wet from rain. V. had placed it there to dry out, and I went and took photographs of it soggy and splayed. The next morning, she went to take it out and noticed words and letters were stuck to the bottom of the tub. She cleaned them off using foam spray, a sponge and some hot water. She placed the magazine on the table. The pages were crumpled and misshapen.

After she was done cleaning, she came out and sat with me and we went slowly, very slowly, through the wet pages looking for cartoons. She said it was like an old book; she had to be very careful with each page. It was ugly now, she said, but she also liked it, and she wanted to use it for something, something that was going to be a secret.

***

Right now, the house looks how I like it. There's a *New Yorker* in most rooms of the house. There's one on the coffee table, one next to the big chair, one next to my bed, and one in the bathroom. I like seeing them open and around. It makes me feel like I'm connected to the pages themselves, to the authors, their words, to New York.

***

Last night, when I was trying to read *The New Yorker*, V. wanted my seat so she could make a fort. This would have been fine with me if I hadn't already been moved from a previous location for fort making. I was then sitting on the couch and trying to read an essay—I think it was by John McPhee or maybe it was about Wendell Berry. I had just become comfortable when she asked for my seat cushion. I stood my ground. I dug my heels in. I said you can take what is around me, but you cannot take this cushion. She continued to ask. She needed it for her fort, and I decided I needed to finish the article before she could move me.

She asked how long that might be, how long that might take, if I had finished yet, when might I get through it. I was frustrated and angry with myself for being frustrated: what was the big deal? The kid just wanted to build a fort. The more she asked when I might be done, the less I could read. The chair I'd previously been sitting in was still available. I could have moved back there, but I wanted to prove a point about my place, about my time, about my comfort. Instead of battling, I ended up telling her I was frustrated, and she understood. She stopped asking. It felt like the biggest deal until it felt like nothing at all.

***

I was prepared for these sorts of battles when we moved in together, and I am surprised that there have not been more moments like this. I imagined more fights for attention. More discussion over who owns what and whose is whose.

Perhaps it was that the house was being built all around us as we built ourselves into who we were together, into this new family, into this new orientation. It hasn't been easy or simple. I can't know, and will never know, what it has been like for two children to live with a new person who has needs and difficulties and thrills and joys.

What I do know is that I never expected this moment: the other day, I came back from the bathroom to find V. and B. sitting on the bed, looking at the caption contest in the back of *The New Yorker*, laughing. Then A. came in and joined them, snuggling up to his dad and sister. And eventually, I did, too.

# After Apples

When I was a kid, apples were one of the fruits I enjoyed, and I liked them every kind of way: whole, sliced, with or without peanut butter, on a small plate, or in my hands. Pink Lady. Granny Apple. McIntosh. Red Delicious.

When I first moved in with B. and his kids, I was confused about their eating habits. For one thing, they didn't eat apples. But it wasn't just that they didn't eat apples—they didn't really eat any fruit. I knew vegetables were a tough sell for kids, but fruit? Apples?

***

I have been writing about apples for months, and every few weeks, I look up the same question: Can you grow an apple from an apple seed? The answer is not really. You can grow an apple from an apple seed, but you will not produce the same type of apple. Instead, you must graft the apple tree.

Grafting is not what I think of when I think about apples. When I think about apples, I think of Johnny Appleseed and see the seeds falling out of his pockets. I hear the song: "Oh, the Lord is good to me / and so I thank the Lord / for giving me the things I need / the sun and the rain and the apple seed." When I hear it, I hear the joy, and the childishness, and the myth we built around him: "...and every seed I sow will grow into a tree!"

***

I started writing about apples days after Roe V. Wade was shot down. I was thinking about bodies and desire and what women are allowed to want: to naturally reproduce children but not do it wildly, as in: no seeds spilling out of pockets. And yet, even to bear your own child is also not so simple. The apple does not simply fall from the tree.

The month I started writing this essay, we were a year into trying to conceive but hadn't yet, and I felt split in two. I lived with two children; I wanted my own.

***

Apple trees are built to deliver children mysterious and undecipherable, which is perhaps why they are often depicted as dangerous.

Take Snow White; in the original version of *Snow White*, Snow White's mother gives her a poisonous apple, and she falls into an endless sleep. In the Disney version, they changed the mother from being her biological mother to stepmother, assuming audiences would not take well to a "real" mother's fear of her daughter's beauty. In both, the apple is a sign of danger and a symbol of desire; the apple is poisoned because the mother wants what she cannot have.

Then there's the almost too obvious to even mention. Eve and her apple and its danger, her temptation to eat the fruit linked to a longing for knowledge. The original sin.

And then there's the teacher and the apple perched on her desk. The teacher is not identified with the apple because she wants more; the teacher is aligned with the apple because she controls its knowledge. She is not to be confused with Eve! God no. She is not tempted by the apple. She's not tempted by anything! She is the chaste guardian of it.

She's a part of me, too. Most days. The teacher. The one with the apple on her desk. An acceptable version of a woman. Those who can't bear, teach. Or those who teach can't bear. Isn't that the saying?

***

This is how one story about apples goes: My father used apples to quit drinking. He was an alcoholic, and he lived in Ireland where his mail was delivered to a bar. At some point, he decided to quit drinking, and he ate an apple every time he wanted a beer. No AA. No therapy. No crisis of faith. No rock bottom. Just apples. Green apples were always what I pictured, but I am not sure if they were. I only know what I've imagined—him wandering the streets of Dublin with a bag of apples and eating them like candy to stave off desire, long before I was born.

Eating apples as a way to restrict oneself from something is a fantasy I'm attached to. Last summer, a man on the radio said he lost weight using apples. He ate an apple whenever he wanted another kind of snack, and it worked. He lost thirty pounds using apples! This man was on the same app I used when I started eating more and more apples. I did not, have not, will not, lose thirty pounds, but I did and do eat a whole lot of apples.

Part of my desire to lose weight was to conceive. I remembered a friend of mine said her doctor told her to lose five pounds when she was trying to have her second child. It sounded absurd at the time—this woman was already as healthy as she could be—and five pounds? What was five pounds to an embryo? But it had stuck with me: to have a baby meant to shed some weight. And so, every day, for over a year, I was eating an apple between most meals. It worked. The weight, I mean. I lost some of it.

***

We live less than fifty miles from the Everglades, where an inedible apple grows. The apple is referred to as the swamp apple, and it looks more like a pear. The last time we went to the Everglades, I tried to capture the fruit in a photograph. I wanted to remember these apples that grow in water full of salt, snakes, alligators, orchids, and sawgrass, and I wanted to have the picture to prove it. But the apple was hard to capture; its green was the same green that surrounded it. It blended right in.

***

I grew up in the Northeast where my mother would make homemade applesauce at the start of fall. The apples she used were not store-bought apples for eating; these were wilder apples from trees around family property. When she made the applesauce, she always kept the skins on, and she cut the meat away from the core with a kind of gentle forcefulness, a kind of secure grace.

My mother still makes applesauce. She has a big cone-shaped strainer with small holes and a round wooden stick. Every fall, she gathers the apples, she cuts the pieces, and she places them into boiling water. Once boiled, she put it all into the strainer over a large bowl. She then presses, and their bright insides ooze. The color is pink, and I like eating it fresh.

When I told her about the kids and their eating habits, she suggested applesauce. Everyone likes applesauce, she said. No, I said. I couldn't imagine it.

***

I have a hard time describing what role I play in my household. I say I live with my partner and his two kids, and then later, in conversation, people will refer to those kids as my stepchildren, and I will feel strange. When people say it, I feel a stop in my chest, a kind of block. Is it because I want them to be my children or because I know they aren't?

When I first moved in with B. and the kids, those same people would tell me I was lucky. One friend who was struggling to get pregnant couldn't get over my good fortune. She didn't say it, but what I heard when she spoke, sometimes overdoing it with the tone of her voice, the pitch of it at a higher octave: "You got to have kids without any of the work."

These were people who were trying their best to make me feel not just comfortable in my new life but also celebratory about it. I was both with them and not. I was lucky, and I was grateful. I am still. But living with the kids did not replace the longing I'd been too scared to mention: I wanted to have my own child, too.

***

In the late 90's and early 2000's, a few movies came out centered around "keeping the baby." One was *Juno*, another was *Knocked Up*, and another, *Friends With Kids*, was about two friends who decide to have a baby together and then fall in love. In each of these films, the baby solves a greater problem. In *Juno*, the baby is adopted into a kind family that Juno is enamored with. In *Knocked Up*, it is the centerpiece for the relationship to inevitably bloom. In *Friends With Kids*, the baby creates their love.

I was young and questioning and political when I saw *Juno*, and it disturbed me. Juno decides first to get an abortion. The camera follows her past an anti-abortion protestor to the receptionist, playing a Nintendo DS. When she sits down to fill out the form, she notices other women, all of whom are tapping their fingers. The camera zooms in on the hands, and the audio of the drumming fingers builds to a crescendo. She runs out of the clinic. She decides to have the baby.

I raged about Hollywood's representation of abortions at the dinner table. I was convinced the religious right had been behind the movie; it was a perfect subterfuge, the way the messaging had infiltrated through what was meant to be a hipster film about two lost kids and a pregnancy.

I was young and naive and confused when I saw it, enough to believe the biggest choice was whether to have a baby.

***

Years ago, I worked at a school where I shared an office with a woman who loved to pick apples. Every fall, she had to pick apples with her wife and their two kids. Apples meant fall, apples meant harvest, apples meant the change of the season, and apple picking meant a consistent relationship to that change.

When we worked together, I was falling in love with B. I never told her. I used our office to stay late into the evening, hop on video calls, send messages, write lengthy emails, cry, and stay at work until I couldn't any longer. I never told her because my coworker seemed very committed to married life. Her wife was such a great cook. Their boys were happy at school. Her wedding had been the most beautiful day. In the fall, they always picked apples.

A year later, she fell in love outside of her marriage, and it shocked me. It shocked her too, but her commitment to apple picking remained. She now lives with her new partner, and between them, they have four kids. In the fall, they all go to the orchard, pick the apples, and take the photographs. Like me, she left D.C., but instead of going south, she went north, where there are more apples to be had, gathered, and eaten.

***

Since starting the weight loss app, I bring apples to school, and the symbolism is not lost on me; there I am, a high school teacher eating an apple, sometimes with another apple perched on my desk. I usually eat one in the morning when I am ready for lunch but have hours to go; I also eat one right after lunch when I wish I could eat another whole plate of food. Before I was trying to lose weight and before we were trying to conceive, I would eat a piece of pizza where I now insert the afternoon apple.

Sometimes my students eat the apples I bring. In the beginning, I enjoyed the exchange. In particular, one student always asked about the apples and if he could have one. It charmed me because he was a huge mess in so many ways: he never had his uniform, was always late, sometimes hungover, and nearly failed an elective that is famously impossible to fail. I thought it was sweet that he wanted a healthy treat. But over time, it started to grate on me. Couldn't he, just maybe, one time, bring in an apple?

***

The apple doesn't fall far or the apple does fall far: that is the only way people can think about children. Either they didn't or they did. What of all the babies who didn't fall at all? Are they no longer apples? Or are they some other kind of apple? One that never made it. The kind we never get to eat.

The other day, I was telling my students that I lived with two children during half of the week, and one said, “We didn’t know you had kids,” and I said, "Well, I don’t in a way, but I kind of do!” I said I live with them part of the time, and one student asked: “Do you get community service for that?”

In baby apps, they use fruit to show you the growth of your baby. I haven’t made it further than a blueberry. Or was it a raspberry? I never made it to the apple.

***

One of my mother’s best friends eats the entire apple: the core, the seeds, the stem. She says she always has, and she doesn’t understand why everyone doesn’t do the same; it’s all edible, after all. This same woman had her tubes tied when she was in her early twenties. She knew she didn’t want kids, and she says she never regretted the decision. She has been married three times, and she always has two, sometimes three, basset hounds around her.

She’s wrong about the seeds, it turns out. They do have poison. But only if you bite into them. If you swallow them whole, you can have as many as you want.

Over the many years I’ve known my mother’s friend, I’ve only heard her express her frustration at being childless once. It wasn’t when everyone initially had kids. She said she rode the wave gracefully. Now that all her friends were either grandparents or obsessed with becoming them, she was annoyed. They were done. They could live their life as they pleased. And yet, they were restricting themselves. She rolled her eyes as she said it. It wasn't just the progeny but the progeny of the progeny—it wasn't just the apple and the tree but the next apple and its tree.

When she said this to me, she was trying to relate. She assumed that because I don't have a child of my own, it was unlikely I would have a desire for one. She turned to me as if in confidence, as if thinking and knowing or wondering if I'd chosen this path. When she said it to me, I was upset, not just because I wanted to be pregnant and wished I could be an obsessed mother and then a grandmother too, but also because I live with two children who do shape my world.

I think about it now and no longer feel offended; I am simply struck that whatever your choices, there's no way around the question of apples and their trees.

***

I find it hard to read essays I used to gobble right up. These were essays by women about being artists and writers and having children. Some of them chose to, others did not, and most of those essays centered on the choice.

In "The Grand Shattering" by Sarah Manguso, she writes about how she never wanted children, even while pregnant. Then, after having a child, she realized the error of her thinking. By the end of the essay, she asserts that having a child is a shattering—one she wants to both write about and read about, exclusively. She says she wants to read work from authors who chose to open up their bodies to that particular pain and love; the only art that interests her is written by and for people who can love something like their own child, which is to say, have their heart ripped open and pieced back together again.

When I first read the essay, it affirmed something within me I hadn't even yet really affirmed in myself—I did want to experience that pain, that love, that heartbreak, even if I was not yet ready.

Now I read it and realize a million missing pieces and see thousands of missing people: want-to-be-parent-writers who never became parents, writers who became parents and stopped writing, step-parents, aunt parents, uncle parents, grandparent parents, farm parents, apple parents, teacher parents, love parents, dead parents, flower parents.

Another friend of mine described having children in the same way as the writer. He said it felt like his heart was outside of his body, like his nerves were always on alert, as if his whole being was sensitized in a new way. Everything hurt, he said, and everything was beautiful.

Another friend said to me: everyone who wanted children, who truly wanted them, would have them. They would just make it so that happened for them in their life. As if it was easy.

How long does an apple tree produce apples?

***

I did the blood test they tell you to do to see if you're ovulating normally, and the phlebotomist had to stick the needle in twice. I am scared of having my blood drawn. I've fainted before. I always tell them this, as a way to help them help me with my anxiety. This time, it didn't work. My panic fueled hers, and for a week afterward, my arm was covered in a giant, bright bruise, spreading from the elbow into the forearm. She said it was my fault; I didn't drink enough water before, I was too stressed out. Had I had coffee?

What I heard her say was: how do you expect to have a baby if you can't handle this?

***

When I fell in love with B., apples symbolized a lack. In our lexicon of emojis, the tomatoes were our symbol for love. We signed most emails with three tomatoes—our way of saying I love you. But we were also not allowed to love one another, and so it followed that for years, we would often try to control it with words, with images, with anything we could. One day, I suggested we try—for the first of many futile times—to be friends. B. wrote me an email, and signed it with three apples instead of tomatoes, and I wailed.

I wailed because I was hungry. What we'd found in one another fed a part of myself I never knew existed. I was full of desire, more than I'd ever felt, and I was terrified, not just because I wanted a person who already had their own children, but because I wanted a person that much at all.

***

It's strange to have a want you can't control. Sure, we can't control anything, not really, but every day I want an apple and I eat an apple, so there are things I want that I can have.

Perhaps it is even stranger to want what you have but also desire something else, something different. What does it mean to want your own children when you already, in a way, have them? Does that make you some kind of a ravenous, never-satiated, always-hungry, bordering-on-gluttonous woman? The scariest kind of woman you can be?

***

Virginia Woolf had an apple tree outside her window. In her journal, she writes about the apple tree often. She enjoys watching it grow, and her husband is often out there, picking through the apples and carrying them back to the house. Sometimes, the sound of his gathering annoys her; other times, she enjoys the distraction. She writes about seeing the apples full and witnessing them rotting; she writes about watching them before they were even born:

*I am writing this at 10 in the morning in bed in the little room looking into the garden, the sun beaming steady, the vine leaves transparent green, and the leaves of the apple tree so brilliant that, as I had my breakfast, I invented a little story about a man who wrote a poem, I think, comparing them with diamonds.*

***

I'm back on the weight loss app. It's not working this time. I eat the apples. Of course I eat the apples. But my body is not budging. It is taking a stand. It is not interested in shifting down or shifting up or being held to any kind of standard. It is laughing in my face; it says, You can't have it. You keep trying, and it keeps falling through your fingers.

The other day a student of mine said, "I've noticed you always have apples." I said he was right, and another student asked, "But how can you eat so many apples? There are only three types: red, yellow, and green." No, no, no the first boy and I said in a kind of chorus: there are thousands of different kinds of apples!

Lately, though, I've been getting rid of more and more apples. I am less likely to keep them as they start to shrink. I have also noticed a texture on the outside I don't like—a rubbery one, or is it more like plastic? I am becoming more discerning with my apples, and some of them are small enough to throw down into the disposal. Others go right into the trash.

***

On Mother's Day, I looked for poems about the type of mother I am, and the "Poems About Motherhood" section of Poetry Foundation only had poems for: "newborn days," "watching them grow," "children on mothers," "mourning a mother," and "losing a child."

I think some would actually say I count as someone in the final category, but others would say no. No. Of course not. I would have to agree with the latter. I have lost an idea of a child, and there's no category for that either.

***

I shared a draft of this essay with B., and he pointed out I'd made a mistake. In the draft of the essay, I'd said the children never tried my mother's applesauce. The anecdote was a great ending to the section about my mother and the fresh applesauce and her assertion they might like it. If the kids didn't eat it, then there would be a point made about distance, about how my mother struggled to understand my role in these kids' lives, too.

But it actually wasn't true, he said. The kids did eat the applesauce, and then I remembered that they did try it, and V. even asked for more. She became obsessed with it in the way she becomes obsessed with food items: for a forty-eight hour period, long enough for her to get sick of it or, perhaps more accurately, to get sick of the attention it brings—the excitement all adults have in the face of a child eating something healthy.

I was embarrassed I'd rewritten the story that way; I was uneasy about the fact that I did not remember the truth about the applesauce. It made me wonder about my own attachment to narratives about who and what and can be a mother. Perhaps I am missing out on what I have all the time.

***

On my birthday this year, I didn't eat any apples. I brought an apple in my purse just in case, but I knew the day would have some food, or more food than I was used to, and it did. My students brought in all kinds of sweets. Donuts, cookies, and cake. The apple stayed in my bag.

It was my 39th birthday, and I had this feeling that it shouldn't be my 39th birthday. Or I should have done so much more if it was my 39th birthday. I should have given birth to children and a book, definitely the book, at least the book—the one I worked on at the graduate school I went to in my thirties when I was not having a baby but going to school to write the book I don't have. There should be more fruit.

The reality is I do have two children and a book. They just don't look the way I thought they would.

***

I wonder about the poem Virginia Woolf's invented man wrote. The one about the apple leaves, the one comparing them to diamonds. I wonder who the man was and what kind of life he'd led and whether he knew he was looking at an apple tree when he saw those leaves. Was he a man of cities and buildings, a man who barely knew an apple from a pear? Or did he know those same leaves would sit atop a circular apple, and if he did, did he know what kind? Or was his focus less on what would become but instead on what was there: those leaves so brilliant, so green, so glistening, so bright. Just like diamonds.

***

Every month, I churn through the cycle: I plant hope for something I don't yet have next to acceptance for what I do. The thing about time is it does change you. You can't eat apples twice a day every day forever, and the people near you, the people with you, graft themselves into your being.

This March, the kids and I spent spring break together. We were on the same school schedule, and we had long, free days. In the past, these days used to scare me. I didn't like letting them do whatever they wanted, but I was also so terrified of the inevitable rejection when I'd make suggestions for a trip to the beach, a walk, a trip to a museum.

This time, something shifted. This time, I felt less scared, and this time, I knew enough not to suggest an activity solely focused on what I wanted to do. They wanted Jimmy John's, and we centered our days on making it to Jimmy John's.

The first Jimmy John's was in Coral Gables along Coral Way, where chain stores are housed in old, beautiful buildings and banyan trees line the streets. On our way inside, a man was just getting off his shift, and hopped onto his bike, nearly hitting us. I forced a laugh, trying to assert my relaxed, "Isn't life a silly journey?" personality which doesn't always land and is rarely convincing. A. has told me more than once that I am one of the more anxious people he knows. V. often tells me I am "helpful," which I always hear as "hopeful" when it first leaves her mouth, wishing it were the case.

The second Jimmy John's was near the plant store where B. asked us to buy native plants labeled with the image of butterflies and the shape of Florida. We picked Walter's Viburnum and Simpson Stopper and Milkweed. V. sat on the cart as A. pushed it, and we piled plants around her, ones with tiny, round leaves because B. told us they were calming. When we got to the car, we pushed the plants forward and together.

Their order at Jimmy John's is always the same—bread and cheese. A. always asks for the biggest one possible, and V. gets the kid's version of the exact same thing: white bread with provolone thrown right on top. The first time we went there together, I was surprised. This is it? I wondered. How could this be it? The kids were excited for me to try it, though, telling me it was all about the bread. The bread is so good, they said, and so I tried it, and the bread was good, but it was not that good. I feigned enjoyment in the way I feigned so much in those early days, hoping to keep enough of myself at bay so as not to rattle the system.

On our trips, I noticed I neither faked enthusiasm nor dismissed theirs. Something had changed even though their orders did not. We sat quietly while we ate, and then I asked if the sandwiches were good. Yes, they said, emphatically, they were so good, turning to me to ask, "Aren't they so good?"

## Beginnings: A Series of Attempts

When you fall in love with someone and leave the life you've built for ten years to be with them in a city at the bottom of the country, people ask questions:

Where are you?

***

The second time I cried watching *Beauty and the Beast* was when I was in the front seat of B.'s car at a drive-in movie theater in downtown Miami. The kids packed blankets and pillows and made themselves a cozy nest in the back of the car. Eventually, V. moved up and sat next to us in the front seat. I made it through the beginning of the movie dry-eyed, which was a great sign of progress. I was no longer ready to collapse in the presence of a Disney movie. And there really was nothing to cry about! Nothing at all. And then, that damn song with the Beast and Belle singing about the surprise love can be, and whoosh, it happened: I started to laugh. "Are you crying?" B. asked. "Yes!" I said, and V. put her small hand on my shoulder, "It's OK," she said, as if she understood, and I think she did.

***

One summer, my cousin and I played a game of Monopoly that went on for days. We hid money in various stashes in places around the house and kept the game going as long as we could. This was one of the only times I remember loving a game because it was not about the game. Instead, it was about a storyline we invented—two young girls with piles of money under beds and chairs and dressers, trying to figure out how to trick the other into thinking it was our last stash.

What made it fun was not the way we'd stuck to the game but how we broke it apart, prolonged it, and tucked it into every crevice.

***

The house in D.C. was broken into while we were on vacation with M.'s family in Martha's Vineyard. They searched through closets, drawers and rooms, and stole M.'s computer, his camera, and a couple of bags.

Two summers earlier, our rental car had been stolen in Vancouver. We spent a day between the police station and the rental car company, trying to find a missing car that wasn't even ours.

When we were in Vancouver, we were a year into marriage and in love in a new way; we were stable and fully synced. We wanted to go to the same restaurants, explore the same places, and lean towards one another's desires. If M. wanted to get on boats, we got a kayak, we found a motorboat, we traveled by ferry, looking for whales and landing on empty beaches. If I wanted to read and write, M. joined me or chose to go his own way; both, a gift. There was no arguing about what to do or where to be. We'd taken the number of trips one takes with a person to learn the dance, and we were great at it.

A year later, in Martha's Vineyard, all I could think about was B. I wondered how the trip would be with him instead; I imagined the ways he would have grabbed me and held me and even pulled me in to kiss me; I wondered how he might come over to ask to see the photographs I was taking. Every way I saw, I wanted him to see, and every place I was, I wanted him to be: standing there with me as fog covered the field, holding my hand still as I took pictures of droplets of water falling from wild blueberries.

When I could, I stole moments to hunt for him. We were emailing back and forth, but it was not enough, was never enough. I wanted to see more. I looked up his website. I went through his art. I wanted his presence, and I wanted to see his body, his face, his form. In some of his videos, it was possible, and those were the ones I went to most often. There was one where he walks over dunes towards the water with a flashlight. His dog is with him, unleashed. When they make it to the edge, he throws a flashlight in Lake Michigan, and it bobs up and down, flashing here and there. The other one I watched over and over was the one where he shatters a crystal glass; in that video, you also don't see his face very closely, but you see the shape of him moving, and you get a close look at his hand.

***

I often wondered if it began with an understanding of pleasure, if it begins with a hunt for it, a lack of it, or a misunderstanding of what it is.

***

My mother recently gave me my grandfather's first book. It was a book of poetry, titled *An End and a Beginning.* It was dedicated to my grandmother during their courtship. The book is small and blue, published through Yale, where he was an aspiring poet. After poetry, he wrote fiction, and after fiction, he focused on nonfiction. The trajectory was not the one he wanted, I've been told, but the poetry, the writing, the way he used words: those stories were always seeped in goodness. When he courted my grandmother, his friends mocked him. They said he could never convince such a beauty to take his hand. My grandmother said she fell in love with his letters, and he must have fallen in love with hers, too, but this is not the story that is so often told.

His use of language is central; his way with words shaped the beginning of it all.

***

Before I even got to the ending of *Middlemarch*, a former professor of mine ruined the ending for me by saying it is a tragedy. She went on: "Everyone thinks the end is romantic, perhaps the start of something beautiful, but in fact, her marrying Will Ladislaw is just another example of Dorothea's naiveté. She thinks her marriage to someone else will be different; what she doesn't know is that it will go the same way. She'll be disappointed, yet again, and the magic will wear right off, as it always does."

***

The other night, B. found me in our bedroom and asked me what I was doing.

"I'm meditating," I said.

He said, "That's not meditation."

"It is."

He explained that my face looked pained: "It's not supposed to be something you have to force yourself to do," he said.

"The thing that keeps people from doing it is the idea that there is a singular way that meditation *should* look," I argued.

"Come with me and lie down here," he said. He moved towards the bed. "We will become the snow fall."

I moved closer: "Okay. I am a snowflake."

"No, no," he said, not a snowflake: "We are the entire snow falling: together, slowly, dropping down."

***

Are you happy now?

***

Not every pain goes away.

People told me it was wild to imagine that was even a possibility.

***

I dream the beginning is the beginning of a self-help book. Or at least a few of those essays akin to the ones in *Cosmopolitan* about how to solve a problem, ones that get to the heart of the matter in five quick easy steps. The problem is the help is always changing. How to help my life at 29 is decidedly different than it is now. Or is it?

At 29, I hadn't read Duras, Davis, or Dickins (still haven't). But I had read Emerson, Emily, and e. e. cummings. My education was good and expensive. It told me: this is all an illusion, question everything, money won't buy you happiness (but it will buy you this education), love isn't easy, beauty is elusive (except in language), and don't take anything for granted. At 29, at 19, in 9th grade, I was armored with what I needed to accept failure and disappointment: all the books and experiments and plays and opportunities had shown me that it didn't always work out, and I could help others to see the same.

And yet, the lessons don't quit. When I was eleven, I might have written an essay called: "How to Find Happiness When You Move Across the Country into Your Grandparents' House: The Singing *West Side Story* Story." When I was nineteen, it might have been: "How to Walk El Camino Without Actually Experiencing a Spiritual Awakening." When I was twenty-five: "How to Land a Boyfriend on a Political Campaign." When I was thirty-five: "How to Avoid Two Years of Lost Wandering, Trust Yourself, and End Up Happy and Living Near the Beach."

***

B. would send me mixes for my road trips to authors' houses. In them were songs I'd never heard of, bands I never knew. He crafted his digital mixes like I remembered doing with cassette tapes: each song fit alongside the next, each one shared meaning and melody with the one that came before and after. But I had abandoned making mixes years before. After college, I no longer sought new music, and I no longer knew how to make a mix on a platform with no boundaries, with no end.

Now, he continues. Each summer, he crafts a new playlist for the family. Sometimes, I will send one or two songs and see what he can do. One playlist is titled, "Can You Make This Into a Summer Playlist?" V. is now a collaborator. He has been teaching her the art: "Don't put on more than one song from any artist," he says; "Consider the transition," he says; "Look for what connects one song to the next to the next to the next."

***

"We've been through so much," B. said.

We were driving towards the house he'd bought in Miami. We had an air mattress on the floor and buckets for tables. Rarely in those months did we go over what had been because the present needed too much attention. We both had no permanent place to live; we both had lives to rebuild. There was no time for going back and forth about what had occurred, and anyway, we had lived it. There we were, here we were, together. What needed to be covered? Those first months, we lived for the building of the new: finding places to live, pans to cook in, glasses to drink out of, quarters for laundry, good coffee, places to relax, corners for suitcases, and places to work.

I wrote:

*I want to be able to right every ship, and gather every rock, and consider each droplet of water, as it sends itself down the edge of the table, fingernail, and wall.*

***

For years, I thought I saw people having affairs everywhere. It reminded me of the Hugo Williams poem, "Saturday Morning"—where "Everyone who made love the night before / was walking around with flashing red lights / on top of their heads...a small price to pay for what [they] knew." The people who were having affairs were tucked into side streets, stopped in their tracks and smiling into their phones. They were texting lovers on planes. They were whispering to one another at bars. They were crying in bathroom stalls. They were typing emails, talking to friends, and calling their lovers, saying, "Soon, but I don't know when."

***

The hard part about finding the beginning is that for so long I was focused on the end. I'd been shocked by endings, and I didn't want to be shocked by the ending of my own marriage, at least not any more than I needed to be. I thought if I could think through enough of the ways it might end, then perhaps it wouldn't be so painful, perhaps I could figure out a way to make none of it hurt, not really, not as much as I was afraid of.

***

I now know I know nothing. In fact, it's never been about the knowing. If it had been, it would have been so much easier. I would have thought my way out.

Or would I have thought my way in?

***

The memories pile up like books on a bedside table. They make their way on top of one another without order. They do not create a linear path. The book on the bottom is not the first memory; in fact, it could very well be the end, and the beginning could be trapped in the middle. They are pieces in a Jenga set, moving around according to what caused the memory. The cause could be anything. A photograph, a question, an attempt at a beginning. The piece is moved and placed on top of another, creating new shapes and precarious holes in the process, teetering before it falls.

I'd like to say that time heals, but that would be false. Time warps, time edits, time slices, and time persists. Better to say time is a sculptor, and its hands are many and free.

***

I asked my students to write about endings this year. I asked them what they thought about them. What did they feel when they saw the word? Some were literal in their approach: *If an experience is bad, then I like it when it ends. If it is good, I am sad when it's over.* But others took different angles, considering the starts embedded in the ends. They became young philosophers, wondering how one begets the other.

***

It's so easy to flip to the back of the book. All it takes is a thumb flipping through pages. All it takes is a hand.

The beginning? It takes a different kind of work. You have to hold the book with two hands, you have to use both—one to open the cover, the other to cradle the end.

***

We live in a house surrounded with Birds of Paradise plants over twelve feet tall and huge palm trees that drop coconuts into our backyard. Our neighbor has a mango tree, and it drops mangoes onto the back patio. If they aren't too badly bruised, we can eat them fresh.

Cutting the mango is still something I am working on. I imagine it is a skill passed down through generations of people who live in tropical places, where mangos have plopped into their backyard for hundreds of years. Perhaps a grandparent shows a grandchild how to cut the mango the way that it's always been done in their family, and then that child grows up to teach the next, over and over and over.

But for me, cutting the mango is a messy battle. I cut around the edges, removing the skin. Then, I cut away the fruit: first, from the easy sides, and then, from the parts where the seed sticks out like an elbow. I continue to cut, as the juice covers my hands. I get greedy and go for more as it slides around, the knife getting as close to seed as I can. The fruit becomes sinewy.

Usually, I eat a piece or two as I go, getting hungrier with each cut. The fruit is soft, tangy and sweet, the flavor of something new, and year after year, it starts to taste more like home.

# Acknowledgements

Thank you to Michael Wheaton, and the entire team at Autofocus, for giving this work its new beginning; I can't tell you how much it has meant to me to watch this work become a book. To the editors and journals who took many of these essays originally, I am forever grateful for the buoys you provided, specifically the editors at *West Branch, Rejection Letters, AGNI, Washington Square Review,* and *Los Angeles Review.*

Thank you to my parents, Michael Gill and Betsy Gill, for supporting me in every endeavor, traveling alongside me, and being willing—and enthusiastic—participants in all my work. Most of all, thank you for teaching me that a home is any place where the people you love are.

Thank you to my siblings, Charles, Annie, and Biz, for being my favorite people to celebrate with and learn from; I admire each of you. Your creative spirits give me confidence in my own.

Thank you to my friends, family, and mentors, many of whom gave me trust in these essays with their edits, encouragement, and insights: Shauna Barbosa, Caroline Falzone, Shilpi Malinowski, Mary Ruefle, Megan Mayhew Bergman, Shara Lessley, Cooper Mitchell Rekrut, and Nora Feely. To Sue Rainsford and Dinah Lenney, who read multiple iterations of this book—your patience, feedback, and generosity made this a truer book. I am lucky enough to have Gillian Linden as friend and family: her writerly wisdom and sharp observations, along with her unwavering support, convinced me I had a story worth telling. Finally, Chelsea Hodson jumped in when the book was almost in the drawer and helped it find its way back into the world, and for that, I cannot thank her enough.

I am thankful for every friend who entered my house and welcomed me into theirs during the years I was writing these essays; in particular, Alex Smith opened his doors countless times and even took the wheel when I needed it most. I am also indebted to the group of friends I created a life with in D.C., who have given me some of the best memories—and moments—of my life. I am grateful to the friends and literary communities that swooped me up when I landed in Miami; notably, the O, Miami organization and its tendrils of fantastic writers and creatives, who have given me a voice alongside theirs.

Finally, this book doesn't exist without Ben; thank you for building a home where love grows, creativity comes first, and beauty abounds. Your love, your care, your eye, and your edits are on every page, and living with you is a daily lesson on what it means to live as an artist. Thank you, always, for saying "yes."

To Veda and Archer, who welcomed me into your lives and let me watch you grow—you've shown me what it means to be a family, and Lemon Drop is home because of you.

## About the Author

Laura Childs Gill is an author and teacher living in Miami, Florida. Her essays have been published in *AGNI, The Los Angeles Review, West Branch, Washington Square Review, and Electric Literature,* amongst others.

— also from Autofocus Books —

*Duplex* — Mike Nagel

*XO* — Sara Rauch

*Until It Feels Right* — Emily Costa

*Cleave* — Holly Pelesky

*Nextdoor in Colonialtown* — Ryan Rivas

*Too Much Tongue* — Adrienne Marie Barrios & Leigh Chadwick

*Picture Window* — Danny Caine

*the nature machine!* — Tyler Gillespie

*A Kind of In-Between* — Aaron Burch

*How to Write a Novel: An Anthology of 20 Craft Essays About Writing, None of Which Ever Mention Writing* — ed. Aaron Burch

*Hiraeth* — Mistie Watkins

*That Spell* — Tate N. Oquendo

*My Modest Blindness* — Russell Brakefield

*A Calendar Is A Snakeskin* — Kristine Langley Mahler

*Culdesac* — Mike Nagel

*Razed by TV Sets* — Jason McCall

*In the Away Time* — Kristen E. Nelson

*The Body Is A Temporary Gathering Place* — Andrew Bertaina

*Daughterhood* — Emily Adrian

*A Healthy Interest in the Lives of Others* — Teresa Carmody

*Leave: A Postpartum Account* — Shayne Terry

*Yes I Am Human I Know You Were Wondering* — Erin Dorney

*Organic Matter* — E.N. Couturier

*If I Can Be Honest: Selected Prose from the Four Years of Autofocus Lit (2020-2024)* — ed. Michael Wheaton

*The Dead Dad Diaries* — Erin Slaughter

*A Revisionist History of Loving Men* — Lena Ziegler

*Marginalia* — Naomi Washer

*The Third Beat* — Lauren Lavín

*Tacoma* — Aaron Burch

*Teen Queen Training: Essays after The Seventeen Book of Etiquette and Entertaining, 1963* — Kristine Langley Mahler

*The Father of the Man: The Last Author Portrait Sitting with Cormac McCarthy* — Beowulf Sheehan

*Discnchanted* — Kaycie Hall